D0467939

MAKING NATIVE AMERICAN HUNTING, FIGHTING, AND SURVIVAL TOOLS

Many people these days enjoy re-creating Native American weapons and survival gear. Randall "Hutch" Hutchison is shown with some of the items he has made to educate both children and adults to an earlier lifestyle.

MAKING
NATIVE AMERICAN
HUNTING,
FIGHTING, AND
SURVIVAL TOOLS

MONTE BURCH

The Lyons Press
Guilford, Connecticut
An imprint of The Globe Pequot Press

The Lyons Press is an imprint of The Globe Pequot Press.

10 9 8 7 6 5 4 3 2 1

Printed in the United States of America

ISBN 1–59228–020-X

Library of Congress Cataloging-in-Publication Data is available on file.

CONTENTS

Contents

ACKNOWLEDGMENTS

I wish to thank Marty Horn, flint knapper and primitive bow-maker, for all his help and for allowing me to photograph him while flint knapping. There is great deal of information, in books and on videotapes, available for the beginning flint knapper, much more than we can list here. One book I would highly recommend, however, is *The Art of Flint Knapping* by D. C. Waldorf.

I would also like to thank Randall (Hutch) Hutchinson for sharing his knowledge and allowing me to photograph some of his work.

Part I

Flint Knapping

Stone has always been a basic material for a variety of tools, beginning with prehistoric mankind, and natural stone was also utilized widely by the Native Americans. Stone was used to create arrowheads, spear points, knives, axe heads, digging tools, food preparation tools, and hide scrapers as well as for personal adornment such as beads, pendants, and necklaces. The types of stone utilized varied according to the locale, but some of the more easily worked and attractive stones were traded great distances. For instance, obsidian from the Rockies and chert from Tennessee, in

Stone was one of the basic tool-making materials beginning with prehistoric mankind and it was a very important material for the Native Americans. Shown are some artifacts from the author's collection, including hide scrapers, hoes, arrows, and spear points. Some broken points are also shown to indicate different styles and sizes.

Flint knapping is a fun and interesting hobby practiced by many modern-day primitive weapons collectors, builders, and hunters.

the form of finished tools or raw materials, was traded across thousands of miles. The art of creating tools from stone, called "flint knapping," is universal to all races of mankind. The term originated in England, where those who made flints for guns were called "flint knappers." The source probably dates even farther back in time, though, to Germany, where the word *knapp* refers to chipping off pieces of stone.

The art and skill of flint knapping has become extremely popular with many people who wish to learn ancient skills. In fact, flint knapping has become so popular that clubs and informal gatherings are increasingly common. The work of many of today's flint knappers is as beautiful, as well as useful, as those made by the ancients. But I warn you: this fun practice is addictive. With a pile of rocks near my back doorstep, I frequently find myself stopping to flake off a chip or two, even when I should be doing something else.

Chapter

1

MATERIALS

Before flint knapping you first need the raw material: stone. Although working with stone is called flint knapping, even the experts argue as to what constitutes "flint." Both old and new world peoples used flint, in its many varieties. Flint, also called "chert," is basically a variety of quartz. Pure quartz is made up of silicon dioxide (SiO_2), but it usually contains certain impurities. Because of the impurities, it has a wide range of colors, from white to gray to green, yellow, brown, smoky black, and blue. Flint is 100 percent quartz, while chert is usually less pure, about 90 percent quartz, but more readily found in many locales. Chert is found in several types of deposits, most commonly along with dolomite and lime-

Modern-day flint knappers have the same basic materials to work with as did their ancestors. A wide variety of stone materials can be used for knapping. Shown here is one of the author's "stone piles."

Chert (sometimes called "flint"), in many of its different varieties, is one of the most common knapping materials. A good geology book is invaluable for identifying the materials.

stone. The deposits include nodules, lenses, and beds. Nodules are roundish balls located in limestone. They have an outside layer called the "cortex," which resembles rough tree bark. These nodules may range from about the size of an egg up to longer than a foot in diameter. Another type of nodule is the lens-shaped. They look more like the cross shape of a lens and they range from very small to some that are a dozen feet or more in length and several feet across. Chert beds consist of a layer of chert, the deposit varying from thin to many feet thick and sometimes miles long. Flint and chert, however, are not the only materials that can be

Chert is found in a variety of different types of deposits. Nodules are roundish balls with an outside bark-looking layer called the "cortex."

used for stone tools. Other lithic stones include jasper, agate, petrified wood, chalcedony, and pure quartz. Jasper is similar in appearance to flint. It is typically reddish orange or yellow because of its high iron content. It's found in both sedimentary and basalt, or volcanic, rocks and is found over much of the North American continent. Agate, which was often used by the Native Americans of the Northwest, is a very colorful stone with varying bands of color. Petrified wood or fossil replacements occur where organic matter is layered between sediments of lava and ash. They are also very colorful, but found mostly in the West. Petrified coral, from Florida, is another fossil material that can be used for knapping. Chalcedony is a form of quartz that is very smooth and has a sort of waxy feel. It can be transparent or translucent and comes in several

Chert is also found in another type of nodule called a "lens" because of the flattened appearance.

Chert is also found in beds or layers.

Other lithic stones used for napping include jasper, agate, petrified wood, and quartz. Shown is a broken "found" quartz point.

colors from white to gray, brown to black. Straight quartz, either clear "rock crystal" or brownish "sugar quartz," was also a popular material with the Native Americans of the West Coast. Other names or materials include: quartzite, opal, sard, basalt, horntel, limestone, metabasalt, metarhyolite, and prase.

A very popular material west of the Rockies and traded greatly is obsidian, or volcanic glass. Most obsidian is black, but browns, greens, and blues are also found. Obsidian is translucent. Although not a mineral or mineraloid, obsidian has a composition similar to granite. It does not fracture in the same manner as the flints, and lends itself to the sharpest edges you can create with knapping. It is fairly easy to work and great for the amateur knapper.

Whichever stone you choose, it must be fine grained without fractures and when struck it should break like glass with a conchoidal structure, which looks like concentric circles or clam shell–like scar patterns. Of course, one of the most unusual materials of the Native Americans was glass, often from milk bottles. Another favorite source was the red glass lenses taken from railroad switch standards. Your favorite beer or wine bottle glass can even be used for knapping.

FINDING THE MATERIALS

You can usually find some sort of natural stone suitable for knapping in almost any region of the country. One tactic is to locate literature describing the geological formations in your state or area. This information is available from the U.S. Geological Survey or, in most cases, from your local County Extension Office. Some excellent natural stone sources in many areas are streambeds, ravines, or gravel beds where stones eroded from banks and other areas may have been washed. Road cuts and construction projects can also provide good sources. With the growing popularity of flint knapping, you can also often trade or purchase raw materials at rendezvous, or from other primitive weapons aficionados. Of course, in order to find the materials you must be able to identify the various types of minerals and stones. A number of good books have informa tion on minerals in-cluding the *Golden Field Guide to Minerals of the World.*

Half the fun of knapping is hunting for the materials. Cut road banks, eroded creek banks, gravel banks, and worn-out eroded pasturelands, all offer good prospecting possibilities.

Minerals vary in their degrees of hardness, and they all fracture differently. "Hard as a rock" is indicative of many flints. On the other hand, some, such as chalcedony, have a softer, more "predictable" fracture. The cherts fall somewhere between. Rated on the Mohs' scale, the most common measure of a mineral's hardness, talc is the softest at 1, quartz is 7, and diamonds are 10. The softer, more predictable stones are the easiest for knapping and also produce the most consistent tools. It's extremely frustrating to work a point for some time, only to have it fracture in the wrong place and ruin the piece. But it happens, even to the experts, especially with some of the harder minerals.

WATER AND HEAT-TREATING

One ancient method of making a stone more workable was to soak it in water. Soaking fills the spaces between the crystals to some degree, with some stones, and provides more pressure when the stone is struck. Soak the stones in a bucket of soft water for a few days before working with them. A process used in some instances by the Native Americans and even more so by today's knappers is heat-treating the stone. Heat-treating does make many of the harder stones easier to work, but it can ruin some of the softer stones. You will have to experiment to determine whether it works with the stones you have. The first step is to attempt to flake without any heat-treating. If the stone is too hard to work easily, you then should consider heat-treating.

Two theories are given for the advantages of heat-treating. First, heating remakes the crystals into a more uniform, denser form. This allows for greater consistency in creating flakes, creates longer flakes, and, because the material is denser, requires less effort in creating flakes. Another theory claims that heating creates microfractures of the crystals and the matrix surrounding them. This in effect weakens the stone to give it more workability. Not all stones need heat-treating. And, in some cases, you may

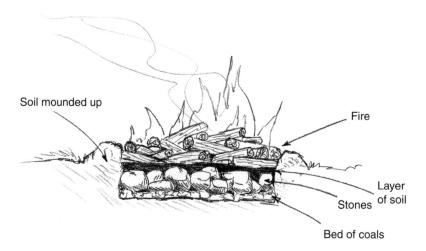

Many stones were "heat-treated," even by the early Native Americans, to make them more workable. A fire pit is the simplest method.

lessen the workability of the stones by heat-treating. It's a good idea to first experiment with the stone to see if the treatment is needed.

Stone can be heat-treated in several ways, from the ancient method of in-ground pit heating to using your roaster oven. The Native Americans heated rocks in pits dug in the ground, and this is still a fairly easy method of heat-treating. You will need a good supply of dry kindling and wood for the fire, as well as a safe place to burn it. Dig a pit about 8 inches deep and as wide as you have rocks to fill it in one layer. It should be at least 3 foot square in order to build a fire hot enough for heat-treating. The soil removed from the pit should be mounded around the edges of the pit. Build a fire in the pit and allow it to burn for several hours to dry out the soil. Then place the rocks in the pit and cover them with 1 inch to 1½ inches of soil. Tamp the soil down solidly over and around the stones. Use the soil around the pit to create a dam to hold the coals in place. Start a new fire on top of the tamped soil. Keep adding wood until you get a good bed of coals up to the edges of the soil dam. As the fire burns, keep stirring it to bring up new materials. After six to eight hours of burning you should have a bed of coals about 6 inches thick. Maintain this until it's time to go to bed or about ten at night. If you've prepared the fire pit properly, the fire should burn all night, with hot coals still remaining at daylight. If the fire goes out overnight, you may need to rebuild it for a few hours. The biggest mistake many make is trying to uncover the rocks and look at them before they are allowed to cool properly. This can result in the breakage of many of the rocks. Allow the pit and rocks to cool for at least two days and then scrape away the ashes. If the soil covering the rocks is still hot, wait another day. If the soil is cool, you can remove the soil and the stones. You should be able to reach heat-treating temperatures of 600 degrees Fahrenheit with this method.

If you don't have a safe place to burn in the open, an alternative is to partially bury a steel drum with the bottom cut out. Place sand in the bottom of the drum; add the stones, a layer of sand, and then the fire. You can use charcoal briquettes or wood; wood, however, makes the hottest fire. A steel top can be used to keep the sand dry when not in use, or as a rain cover when in use.

Some knappers have also used crock pots as well as roaster ovens for heat-treating some of the mid-range hardness stones. Do not, however, use a microwave. It can cause the stone to heat too fast, creating the danger of explosion.

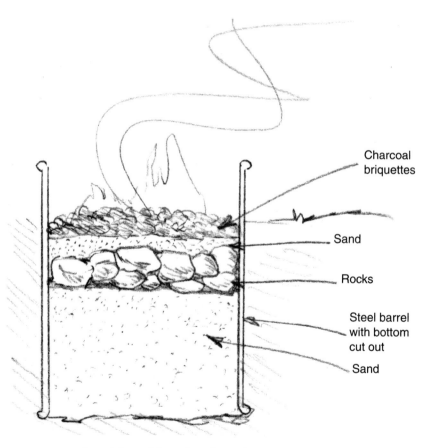

A steel drum with sand can be used to contain the fire.

One of the most popular methods of heat-treating is with a ceramic kiln. Ceramic kilns allow for slow heating, extremely high heat for treatment of even the hardest stones, and the ability to very slowly heat-treat to specific temperatures. The method is simple: the stones are stacked in the kiln, and then the temperature is raised slowly, about 75 degrees Fahrenheit per hour, until the desired temperature is reached. For example, 650 degrees Fahrenheit is a typical critical temperature for mid-range materials such as Burlington chert. Hold the temperature for four to six hours, then turn off the kiln and allow the materials to cool slowly.

One technique is to double-heat the harder stones. First, heat the unbroken stone. Then chip off blanks to be used for blades or points and reheat these.

An excellent information guide, *Roasting Rocks: The Art and Science of Heat Treating* by D. C. Waldorf provides much more detailed information, including the different materials and critical temperatures, as well as hold times for the heat treatment of stones.

Chapter
2

TOOLS AND WORKPLACE

The ancients and Native Americans used only a few "natural" tools, readily found at hand for knapping, and today's "purists" do the same. Some more modern tools can also be used for some purposes if desired.

Early tools were "natural" tools found near at hand. Today's knappers use many of the same simple tools. Shown are the tools of modern-day knapper, Marty Horn.

HAMMERSTONES

The first and simplest tools are hammerstones. These are typically water-worn stones from a creek, river, or gravel bed that readily fit the hand and are

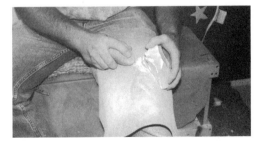

Hammerstones are some of the most common tools. They are typically hard materials used to strike against the work stone. Water-washed, round creek stones are some of the best.

heavy enough to be used as a hammer to break the chert materials into workable spalls (chips or splinters of stone). Hammerstones are typically of granite, quartzite, or other hard materials. You'll need several hammerstones of varying sizes.

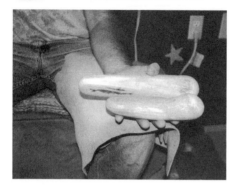

Billets are handled, hammer-like tools also used to strike against the work stone. Native American billets were heavy, thick sections of moose or elk antlers. Modern-day knappers often use brass billets.

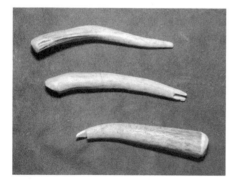

Pressure flakers are used to press against the surface to "pop" flakes. The pointed tines of deer or elk antlers were commonly used. One tip should be extremely fine for chipping off notches. Notched antler tips are also used to "lever" off chips.

BILLETS

A billet is a bone or antler tool used for flaking. Large sections of heavy antlers, such as those from moose or elk, are used to strike the stone spall to knock off chips and shape the edges. Deer antler bases can also be used, but they should be heavy. The cut edges of the billets should be smoothed and rounded where your hand fits to prevent abrading your hand. Some knappers prefer heavy sections of copper for the task, and I've even used a heavy-duty tractor implement pin. But remember, iron and flint produce sparks, which can set off a fire.

PRESSURE FLAKERS

The upper, pointed tine end from deer or elk antlers is used to apply pressure to the edges of the spall to chip off small flakes. The handle ends should be rounded to protect your hand. You will probably wish to have several of these pressure flakers of varying sizes and point shapes. Some modern-day knappers use pointed copper tools for this chore as well. You'll need one flaker with a very sharp and small point for creating notches. Notches can also be shaped with a file.

PUNCHES

Indirect percussion is used in some instances, tapping on a punch to drive off flakes. Punches may be made of antler tips with their ends shaped to create a driving edge, or with antlers tipped with copper.

Punches are struck with a hammerstone to drive off flakes. Old-time punches were antler tips with their edges shaped like chisels. Copper punches were also used. An antler piece with an inset, ground-off nail head makes a very good punch.

ABRADERS

Abraders are extremely important since they are used to shape or smooth a striking platform on an edge. Pieces of sandstone are natural abraders. A section of a broken grinding wheel can also be used.

Abraders are needed to grind a flat edge for striking. A piece of sandstone is a natural abrader.

SAFETY TOOLS

Modern-day knappers also should use safety tools. These include goggles to protect your eyes from flying chips and leather gloves to protect your hands. Many knappers like to use leather kneepads, although I prefer a piece of leather laid over my knee. You will also need pieces of soft leather for holding the stone to be struck. Last, but not least, many materials, such as flint and chert, are silica based. If you breathe the fine dust from knapping, you are in danger of the lung disease silicosis. This can be a serious threat if you do much work indoors or without adequate ventilation. If possible, work outside where a breeze can blow the dust away. If you must work inside, make sure it is a well-ventilated spot and use a fan to blow the dust away. But do not work in an air-conditioned or forced air–heated building; the dust can be sucked into the vents and spread throughout the building, posing a threat to everyone inside. If you really get into knapping, it's best to have a separate, well-ventilated "workshop." To be safe, wear a respirator mask with filter cartridges designed for use with asbestos. And, again, always provide adequate ventilation.

A PLACE TO WORK

Knapping is sit-down work. The Native Americans did it around their campfires. A small stool can provide the modern-day knapper with a comfortable height to position his knee for easy knapping. The workplace can be just about anywhere. My favorite is the back step to my shop. I have a

A comfortable place to sit down and work is also important.

big pile of rocks at hand, out of the way of other activities, and I keep my tools in a leather bag just inside the door. When I feel like chipping away, I reach for my tools, sit down for a bit, relax, and chip. Of course, this only works in good weather. A place indoors, where you can keep a small stool, your tools, and a pile of rocks, works just as well.

Indirect pressure flaking is best done on a solid surface such as a sturdy workbench. The best choice is a bench that's not too low so you don't get a backache from bending over the tedious work.

Chapter

3

BASIC KNAPPING

Don't say I didn't warn you. Knapping is addictive. The basics are very simple, but knapping has many levels and becomes increasingly complicated. For instance, once you master the basics, you'll probably want to try fluting and serrating edges as you explore the craft further. But before you begin, it's a good idea to study other points, whether ancient or modern. Then, for your first attempts, copy some of the simpler designs. Most knappers like to faithfully follow specific styles or regional points, especially since the regional materials will often be more suited to those styles.

TYPES OF KNAPPING

In order to drive off chips to shape the stone, you must first understand that flint or chert has a conchoidal fracture according to the geologists. A cone-shaped chip is removed opposite the point of impact. One example of how this works is when a BB strikes a plate-glass window. The backside of the window will have a cone-shaped opening. Controlling the force, angle, and position of the blows used to create a chip allows you to fracture the stone with some sort of predictable outcome—at least it will once you learn

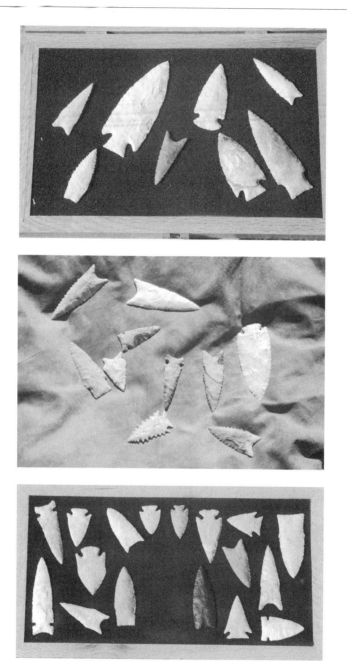

The art of knapping is fun and can become addictive. Shown are some beautiful points made by modern-day knapper Marty Horn.

Point of impact

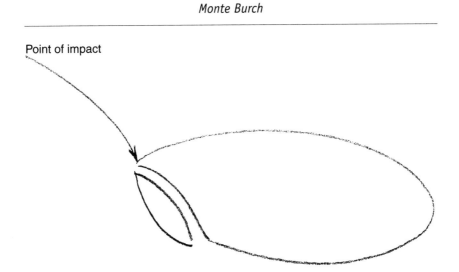

First, you must understand the "physics" of knapping. When stone, such as chert, is struck, a "conchoidal" fracture occurs. A cone-shaped chip is driven off opposite the point of impact in the same manner as when a BB strikes a plate-glass window.

how. This, like many other skills, requires practice, patience, and learning. You will make many mistakes, but you can learn from each and every one of them. Our farm was once a Native American village, probably Osage, and it has lots of flint stones scattered about. We assume it was a major point knapping spot with the points traded to other regions and tribes. We find many points, some broken over time and some that have a few flakes removed from one or two sides, and then broken. My nephew Morgan calls these "#@*% points." He envisions the maker working the point, it breaks, and he tosses it over his shoulder with a few choice words.

The ancient skill of knapping uses three basic techniques for flaking off chips: percussion flaking, pressure flaking, and indirect percussion flaking. These three techniques are used in combination to create most points or tools.

Percussion flaking utilizes a hammerstone or the edge of a large antler or copper billet to strike the edge of a stone to drive

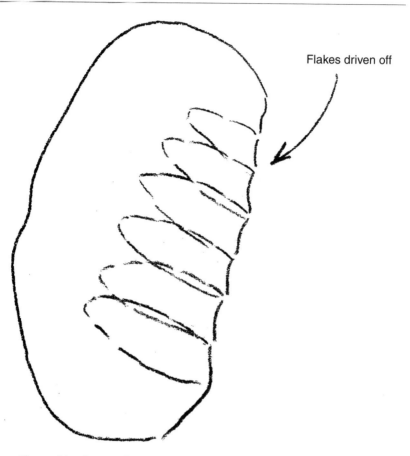

Flakes driven off

The resulting fractures in a stone create a "wavy" appearance in the surface.

off flakes. This is most commonly used to break off a large chip from a stone to begin the point. It is also used entirely for shaping the larger, rougher implements.

Pressure flaking utilizes pointed tools such as an upper tine from an antler or antler tipped with copper. The pointed tool is placed against the "platform" or edge and pressure is applied to drive off the chip. Pressure flaking is the intermediate stage, used to continue to rough-shape and, in some instances, final-shape the implement.

Indirect percussion utilizes a punch placed on the platform or edge. The end of the punch is then struck with a mallet to drive off the flake. Indirect percussion is used for more precise flaking, for instance to serrate an edge or to create a notch.

The wavy appearance of a point or tool is a record of the shock waves generated by the removal of the chips or flakes.

CREATING A STONE TOOL

In most instances, the first step is to drive off a spall from a nodule, lens, or other piece of raw material. Two methods are commonly used. The first is called "bipolar spalling." Position the

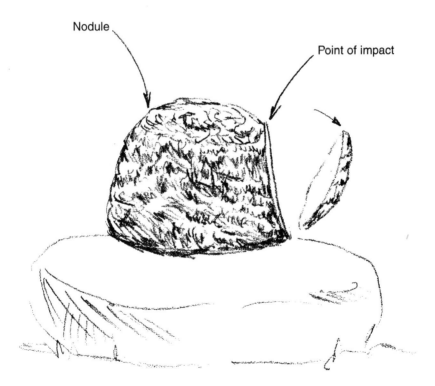

Nodule

Point of impact

The first step in creating a stone point is to drive off a spall from the side of a nodule or other piece of raw material. In bipolar spalling, the stone is placed on another solid stone and a large hammerstone is used to strike the working stone.

nodule or lens on a solid "anvil" of stone or other sturdy surface. Use a large hammerstone to strike directly down on the top of the working stone. This should split the nodule or stone in half or some similar division. In most instances, a smaller piece of stone will be driven from one side. In the case of large work pieces, large hammerstones are sometimes thrown down with force onto the work piece to shatter it into smaller working pieces. The first step isn't necessary if using a purchased or found preform, obsidian, or glass. A preform refers to a blank or spall that has been worked into a rough outline shape from either a spall or whole piece of material.

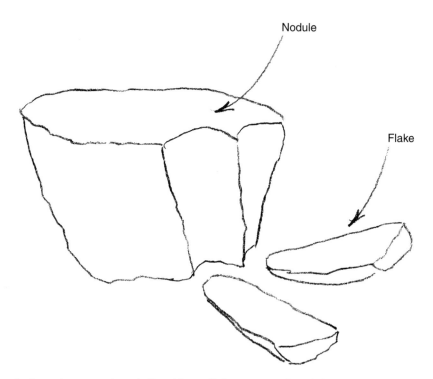

In decapping, an end cap is first driven off the narrow end, and then the newly created "flat" end struck to drive flakes off the side. This creates a work piece from which the point is produced.

In freehand spalling the work piece is held with a leather glove or leather pad in one hand and a hammerstone is used to strike against the edge to drive off a spall.

Another method, called "decapping," is used with large work pieces. An end cap is first driven from the narrow end of the work piece, and then the flat surface is struck down the sides to drive off the flakes. You will probably have to drive off several to get one that will work properly.

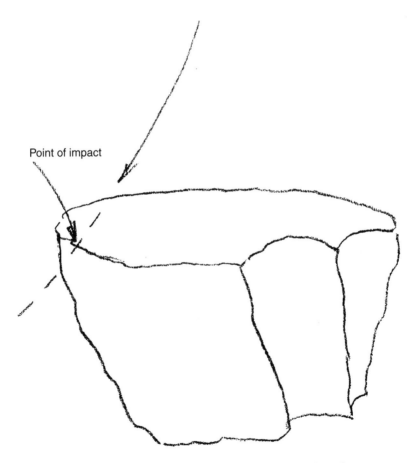

The ideal surface to strike is a 90-degree angle. Grind or abrade the surface to create a good striking surface. Then "swing through" as you strike. Don't stop the striking tool at the edge.

Core

Flake

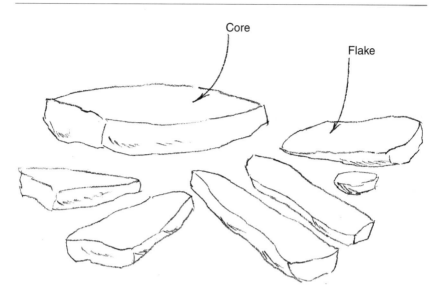

As you drive off work pieces, turn the nodule to work on all sides. You should end up with several work pieces or "spalls." You will probably end up with a flake core, or the center. On large nodules, this core can be used for an axe or blade. On small nodules, this core may be the work piece.

The work pieces will come either naturally or, if you purchase or trade them, in three different shapes: nodules, plates or lenses, or blocks. The method of creating spalls from them is similar, yet somewhat different for each. With nodules you must first chip or grind off the rough outside "bark." The ideal "face" or striking surface should be 90 degrees to the direction of the chip or flake, but this isn't always possible. Some knappers like to break larger nodules in half first, but you may destroy the nodule in the process. Smaller nodules, for the most part, work better than extremely large ones. Grind or abrade the striking platform so it is flat. The grinding will also strengthen it. Remove any overhang by grinding away. Then with the work piece called a "core" either on the stone anvil, in your hand, or solidly supported on the ground, strike the edge of the platform with the hammerstone or billet. You don't want to swat at the edge, stopping the hammerstone on the edge. Instead, envision striking "through the stone." This is the same type of follow-through as with many other pursuits, even wing shooting. If you are supporting the core with an anvil or have it wedged in the ground, make sure there is enough room for the follow-through. The core should, however, be solidly supported. If allowed to move away from the blow, the flake may fracture instead of breaking off cleanly. Once you've driven one flake or spall from the edge, reposition the work piece and strike next to the just-removed flake to drive off another flake. Continue around the nodule driving off flakes or nodules, which will then be shaped into the tool desired. The core left, called a "flake core," is often then shaped into larger tools, such as axes, spears, hoes, and saws.

Lens cores are struck from the narrow end to drive off flakes. On small lens pieces the flakes will normally run the entire length of the lens. The lens may fracture in equal or nearly equal

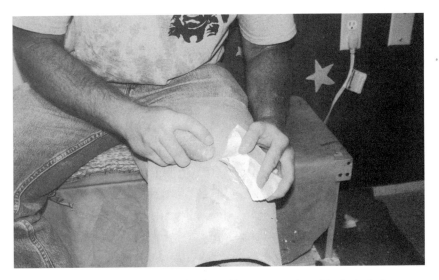

The flakes, spalls, or blanks can now be shaped into any number of tools, including arrow points, spears, knives, axes, and many others.

Stone biface have both edges shaped, as in this arrow point.

parts, or with larger pieces, leave a "flake core" that can also be used for larger pieces.

Slabs are often the most difficult for beginners to work because they tend to fracture more unpredictably—until you learn to identify the pattern. Set these aside and work on them after you gain a little experience.

Regardless of the shape of the core material, at this point you should have a number of flakes or spalls, or blanks, ready to turn into any number of stone tools. These include: arrowheads, spear points, knives, axes, hide scrapers, food preparation implements, and digging tools. Native American artifacts consist of several specific items. A stone biface tool has two faces that have been flaked or worked to create a simple edge. The most common examples of these are arrowheads, spear points, and knives. A stone unifacial tool has only one side worked. This was particularly common with digging tools and hide scrapers. Some simple projectile

A uniface has only one edge shaped, as in this scraper.

points also have only one side worked. Blades can be spear or knife points, and are usually twice as long or longer than they are wide.

Chapter

4

MAKING ARROWHEADS

A rrowheads, or points, are the most common tools made from stone. Even though some states forbid their use for hunting game such as whitetail deer, they are deadly. In some ways, they are even more deadly than modern-day metal arrowheads. Regardless of the style, projectile points such as arrowheads with

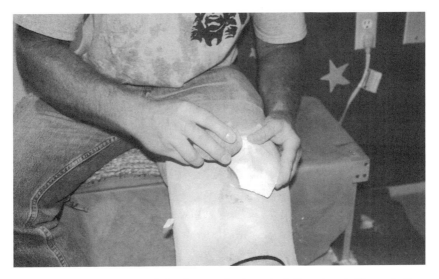

An arrowhead or knife is made by the same basic method. To make a knife, create the spall or work piece as described in the previous chapter.

notches consist of a point, edge, blade or body, shoulder, barb, notch, tang, stem, and base. Simpler arrowheads without notches were often used as well. You may prefer to make a simple straight base point for your first attempt.

The first step again is to drive a flake or spall from the core. (The basic steps are described in the previous chapter.) Small points can usually be made from small flakes driven off the sides of a core after the larger flakes or spalls have been removed. You can also drive smaller flakes or spalls off larger ones to create the arrowhead blank.

Larger blanks can be made into smaller ones with additional percussion chipping. For the most part, however, most of the shaping of the point is done with pressure chipping or flaking. A sharp pointed tool is used to "pry" or "push" off flakes or chips, rather than striking the stone with another tool. The chips are small and are fractured from the opposite side of the blank than where the pressure is applied, again in the conchoidal or core fracture manner. Primary flaking does the rough-shaping of the piece. Some pressure tools can be fitted with a long "crutch" held under the armpit to provide greater leverage and pressure. The blank is held with a leather glove, along with a piece of leather around the blank or over your knee, and the pressure point applied using a pushing, twisting motion. This is where patience is indeed a virtue. Do not attempt to hurry or to remove too much material at a time by removing large flakes. Instead, study the edges and plan your moves before you make them. I'll look at a piece, determining exactly where to strike, but then I may leave it and go about my business. I later come back after thinking about it and making a platform, and then strike it. Experienced knappers, however, don't hesitate.

Once you have the blank or preform, creating an arrowhead, or for that matter knife or spear point, consists of four basic steps.

1. *Rough-Shaping.* The first step is rough-shaping. Square points, round edges, or obtrusions are removed from the edge of the piece using a hammerstone or large billet. Strike a flake from one side, turn the tool, and strike from the other side, alternating to achieve symmetry to the two sides of the tool surface. Once you finish this step, you already have a basic stone tool that can be used as an axe or hide scraper.

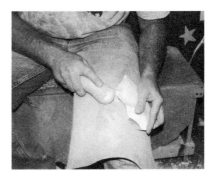

Use a hammerstone or large billet to drive a flake off one side.

2. *Primary Pressure Chipping.* The next step is primary pressure chipping. The edge is shaped and humps and lumps are removed. In this case, the edge must be abraded to create a platform that allows you to drive longer flakes. In most instances, you will need to drive flakes past the centerline of the piece, an imaginary line from the tip to the center of the base, to thin

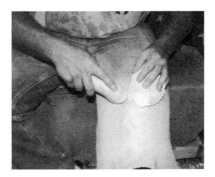

Next, turn the tool and strike from the opposite side of the same edge.

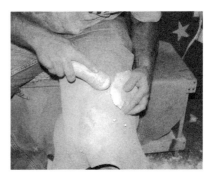

Strike a flake from the other edge side.

the center portion and shape it. When you complete this step, the basic piece should be completed.

3. *Secondary Pressure Chipping.* In this step, the edges of the piece are refined to provide a uniform thickness and shape. Again, platforms must be ground on the edge for each flake in order to continue thinning by driving long flakes off the piece. The idea is to provide a uniform thickness. The amount of effort taken with this step really determines the quality of the piece. In some instances, this may be the final step, for example, if the piece will not have notches in it.

4. *Pressure Finishing.* The final step is pressure finishing. This may entail serrating the edges, fluting the entire piece, and/or cutting notches in the base. A notched antler, or two small antler pieces tied to-

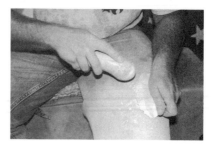

Turn the tool over and strike a flake from the opposite side of the second edge.

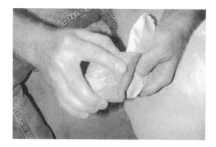

After the tool is roughed-in by percussion striking, the next step is to use pressure chipping to refine the tool shape and edge. The edge must first be abraded to create a straight smooth striking platform. This provides for longer flakes.

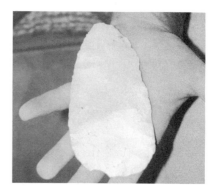

Drive flakes past the centerline of the work piece.

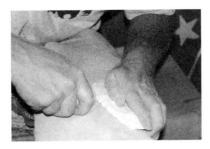

Continue pressure chipping around the work piece until the basic piece is completed.

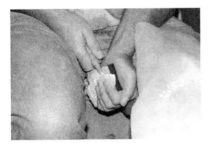

Secondary pressure chipping is used to thin the edges of the piece and provide a uniform thickness and shape. In many instances, once you have a basic shape the piece is finished.

Pressure finishing refines the piece. This may entail fluting the entire piece or serrating the edges. A notched antler can be used to "twist" off the serrations.

gether to create a prong, can be used for nibbling away serrations and working on notches.

NOTCHES

In many instances, such as on some arrowhead and spear point designs, the piece must be notched. Creating notches is an often-daunting task, especially for beginners, and especially on an otherwise beautiful piece on which you have spent a great deal of time and effort. You can and probably will break some pieces creating notches. You should basically have a triangular piece before you begin notching. One trick is to chip off the points of the base corners before attempting to create the notches.

Wedge or edge-pointed pressure tools are used for creating the notches. These can be shaped antler tips or copper-tipped antlers or shaped copper pieces. The pressure tool is pressed in place with a downward motion to remove a chip. The piece is turned and a chip removed from the

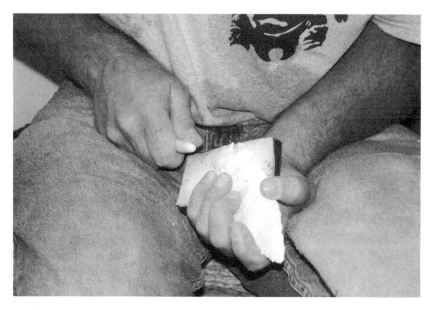

Notches are often created in many arrowhead and spear points. A very sharp pressure tool is used for this chore.

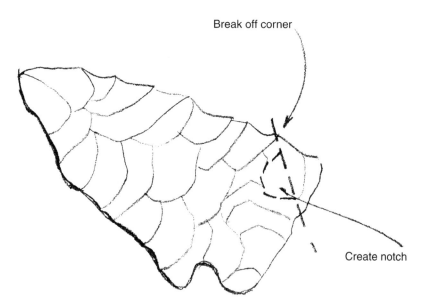

Break off corner

Create notch

It's best to first chip off the base corners before attempting a notch.

opposite side. This is continued until the notch suits. The opposite notch should be shaped at the same time to achieve as much symmetry as possible. A small punch may also be used for indirect pressure flaking to create the notches.

FLUTING

The ultimate in stone working is fluting. This may be a large flute driven off each side of the base of a spear point to fit the shaft of the spear more easily, or the fluting may consist of

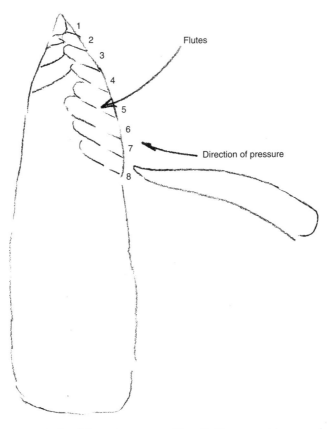

Fluting is the ultimate in stone working. Platforms must be ground on each edge before creating these long chips.

oblique flutes driven from the edge to the center of the piece in a consistent pattern on all four sides. In both instances it takes experience and practice to create. Platforms are always ground in the areas of each flute to allow a long flake.

SMOOTHING

All edges of arrowheads and spear points should be as sharp as possible. Use nibblers or small pressure tools to create a fine, but sturdy, sharp edge. Then, finally, abrade the inside of the notches and the bases of the arrowheads and spear points. This prevents them from cutting the lashings that hold them in place.

Flint knapper Marty Horn likes to finish off his points by melting beeswax, lightly coating the point, and then buffing it well. This not only brings out the color of many stones, but also adds a beauty and luster to them.

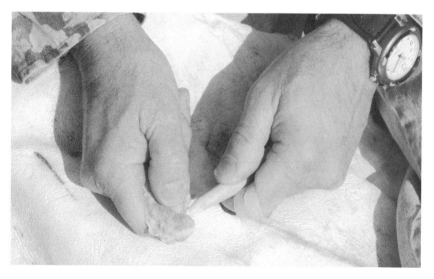

The final step is to use tiny nibblers to smooth and sharpen the edge.

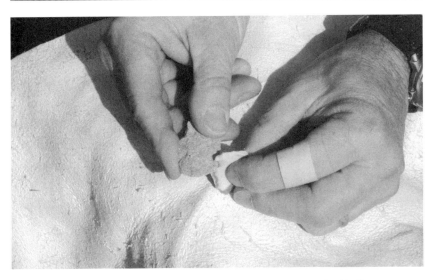

Then abrade the inside of the notches so they won't cut the binding.

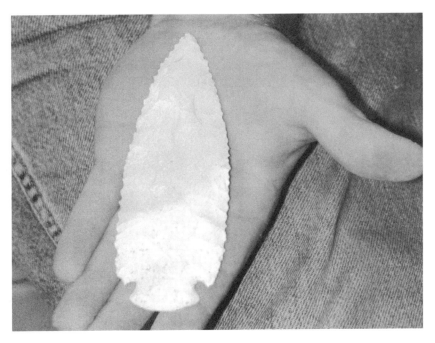

A finished spear point made by Marty Horn.

Chapter

5

OTHER TYPES OF TOOLS

You can re-create or actually create a wide variety of stone tools, following examples from the Native American peoples. But you will need good reference materials. Some examples can be copied from other knappers. Many local museums offer fine examples as well.

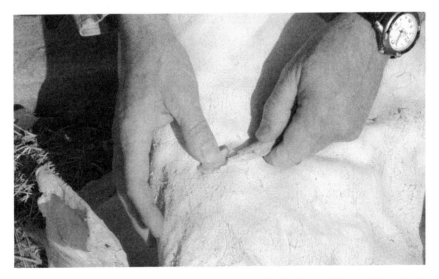

Arrow points are made in the same manner. Although they're smaller, they're actually easier to make because they aren't as susceptible to breaking at the last minute.

Shown are a wide variety of arrowhead styles.

ARROWHEADS

Arrowheads or projectile point artifacts are the most commonly copied items. Many different types have been identified according to age and location. These range from the Clovis, Paleo-Indian points dated from 15,000 to 10,000 B.C. to the later points, which include the Middle Mississippi, Cahokia, Nodena, and Columbia River gem points dated to as late as A.D. 1700. An excellent resource is *The Best From Story in Stone*, a 24-by-36-inch wall poster illustrated by Valerie Waldorf. Full-sized, detailed drawings illustrate the 208 types or type groups from the central and southern U.S. *The Encyclopedia of Native American Bows, Arrows and Quivers* series by Steve Allely and Jim Hamm also illustrate many of the different points.

SPEAR POINTS AND KNIFE BLADES

A wide variety of spear points and knife blades were also produced, ranging from small to large, heavy points. Finding these intact is not as common as finding the smaller points because the larger points and longer blades broke much more easily. The Upper Mississippi Valley (Woodland Culture, 1000 B.C. to A.D. 100) produced many fine spear points and knife blades. The Southeast produced a number of large ceremonial blades, some as thin as a ¼ inch, some as small as 1 inch wide, and some as

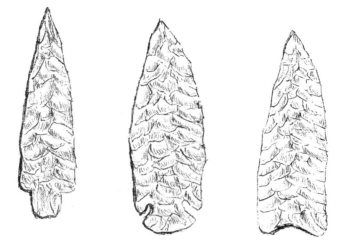

Any number of spearhead styles may also be created, following traditional patterns.

long as 3 feet. Scepters, or hooked blades, batons, and maces were also found in the mounds of the Southeast Native Americans. These represent some of the Native Americans' finest stone artifacts. The Hupa and Yurok tribes also produced extremely beautiful obsidian ceremonial blades.

HOES, SCRAPERS, AND DRILLS

Although less "exciting," many other tools were made of stone. Hoes were quite common in the Southeast, East, and even in some of the Southwest. These larger pieces were usually made of a fine flint. They were hafted either in a straight line or at an angle to the wooden shaft. Hide scrapers and scrapers for other uses were also some of the most common pieces. Many of these were used as is; others were also hafted on short wooden handles, again either in-line or at an angle for pulling or scraping. Small, thin flint drills were also made and hafted into a socket in

Hoes, scrapers, and drills can also be created.

wooden pieces for use in drilling wood, bone, and other materials. Small stone implements were also shaped into chisels to be used in similar ways.

Part II

Arrows

When most of us think of Native American hunting, fighting, and survival tools we think bows and arrows, and there is indeed a great deal of mystique about these war and survival tools and weapons. Many "primitive" weapons aficionados make their own bows; fewer make their own arrows, and even fewer make them in the ancient manner. Making your own arrows and fitting your own handmade points to them, however, completes the Native American and primitive tradition. A well-made arrow, fitted with a stone point can be extremely efficient and deadly. If you have the opportunity to hunt with your own handmade bow, arrows, and points, especially deer or other big game in a state that allows it, you can experience some of the most satisfying hunting ever. If you've had the chance to examine an artifact arrow, or even one made by a serious modern-day, primitive bowyer, you'll often see beauty as well. As with stone points, the Native American tribes made many different types of arrows depending upon region. You may also wish to copy the arrows from your region. Numerous reference books can provide details of the arrow designs from your area. Local museums can also be excellent sources for information.

Chapter
6

MATERIALS

Arrows have and can be made from a number of raw, native materials. Part of the fun of building your own primitive-style archery equipment is looking for materials—it's just another excuse to be in the woods or outdoors. Native American arrows were made from three types of materials: hardwood shoots or sprouts; reeds and cane; and splits from larger pieces of wood.

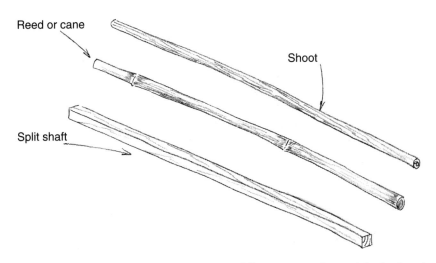

Native Americans arrows were made of three different types of materials: hardwood shoots, cane, or splits from larger wood sections.

SHOOTS OR SPROUTS

The easiest material to use for arrows is a shoot or hardwood sprout. These are basically twigs of wood ⅜ inch or slightly larger, up to ½ inch in diameter and of the length needed. As you can guess, shoots with the most consistent diameter through their length are the best choices. Straight shoots are also important, although they can be straightened somewhat as you make the arrows. And, they must be maintained straight. One of the most common tools was and is a shaft straightener. These are made from stone or a section of antler with a hole in it.

Naturally, wood species that produce the straightest, most consistent diameter as well as the strongest shafts are the best choices. One of the woods most commonly used by many Native Americans was dogwood, which is considered second-story canopy. Its shoots normally sprout in thickets in the deeper woods where they grow straight reaching for sunlight. A dogwood

The most common arrows were made from the shoots of hardwoods, such as dogwood or hazelnut. Choose the straightest shoots you can find.

shoot can also be straightened fairly easily and, for the most part, stays straight. Dogwood is also extremely hard and it polishes to a beautiful smooth finish. In some parts of the country, it is called "red osier."

One shoot I've found to be extremely workable and straight is hazelnut, which was a very common Native American arrow wood. This shrub-type tree grows in dense sprouts. If you find it along the edges of woods or trails, it will be fairly straight in the lengths needed for arrows. It also is commonly found along roadsides, but there the tips often grow downward toward the ground and don't produce as straight a shaft. The different varieties of viburnum were also used, especially in the East, where some varieties were even called "arrow-wood." Chokecherry and serviceberry were also common arrow materials. Elderberry was used to some extent, but with its hollow center, it's fairly brittle. Wild rose, sourwood, and yaupon holly were also used for hardwood shoot arrows. In some instances, two woods were used, joining them together to produce a shaft.

COLLECTING SHOOTS

The best time to collect wood shoots for arrows and other projects is in late winter while the sap is still down. Although all shoots will crack somewhat when dry, those cut in the winter months tend to crack the least. Some woods may not be as easily distinguished without their leaves, so identify and locate the plants in late summer and mark their location for winter gathering. When the leaves are off, however, you can more readily discern the best possible shoots.

Pick the straightest shoots you can find. Gradual bends can be straightened but kinks and sharp bends cannot be changed. Shoots with knots and other deformities will not produce good arrows. Be very selective in your choices—it will more than pay for

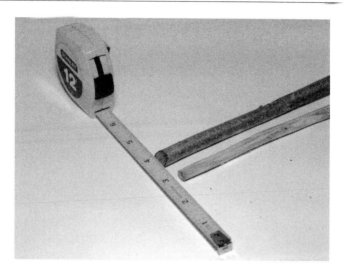

The shoots should be at least 6 inches longer than needed and ⅜ to ½ inch in diameter.

itself in the long run. The shoots should be about ⅜ to ½ inch in diameter and at least 6 inches longer than the desired finished arrow length. This length allows for cutting off split ends and other problems. Also collect a greater number of shoots than you think you'll need. In the process of curing, some shoots may twist and warp, even crack their entire length and have to be discarded. You'll probably end up with only about half the number of arrows as you had beginning shoots.

REEDS AND CANE

Reeds and cane were also commonly used arrow material over much of the United States, but especially in the Southeast. Being hollow and lightweight, yet extremely strong, reed arrows are in fact, somewhat akin to today's modern composite and aluminum arrows. They're fast and light. Several different reed subspecies were utilized. One common reed in my part of the country was

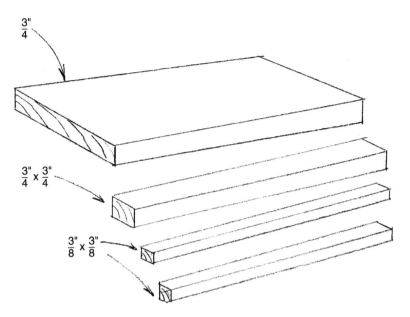

Split timber arrows are cut or split from wood slabs.

called "switch cane." Reeds were often tipped with hardwood to produce arrows.

SPLIT TIMBER ARROWS

Arrows were also made from small-thickness wood pieces split from larger logs or sections of wood. Many woods were used for this purpose, with hickory a very popular wood with many tribes. Ash, birch, oak, and black locust were a few of the hardwoods chosen. Softwoods included Sitka spruce, Douglas fir, and Port Orford cedar. Some of the softwoods are still being used in manufactured split timber wood arrows today.

Chapter

7

MAKING SELF-ARROWS FROM SHOOTS

Shoots, if you can get them, are the easiest to work with in creating self-arrows. Self-arrows are one-piece arrows or arrows made from one solid shaft. Footed arrows are made of two wood species joined to create the shaft.

INITIAL STRAIGHTENING AND CURING

The shafts are cured and straightened in two stages. First, the shafts should be initially straightened. This also allows for further selection or, I should say, rejection of arrows that have kinks or splits. There will be additional straightening processes as you proceed in completing the arrow shafts. The Native Americans often used antler and bone straightening tools, which are nothing more than a piece of bone, stone, or antler with a hole in it. The hole must be slightly larger than the arrow shaft diameter. You can also simply bend the shafts by holding both ends and placing the bend over a solid object such as a table edge. With either method, the shafts must first be heated to make them flexible. Apply a light coating of grease, such as lard or cooking oil, to the shafts. To fol-

Making your own arrows adds to the enjoyment of primitive shooting. And, as you can see from this group of arrows made by Marty Horn, they can be extremely effective.

low the original method, build a small fire with stones on the sides and allow the fire to build a bed of coals. Lay the shafts across the rocks and over the coals, leaving them there just long enough for the shafts to thoroughly heat, but not long enough to scorch them. This takes only a minute or two. Roll the shafts as

The first step is to straighten the shafts. Antler or bone straightening tools can be used.

they heat up, allowing the heat to be evenly absorbed.

Using a pair of old leather gloves or barbeque thermal gloves, remove the shafts and sight down them to locate any bends. Hold the shaft firmly and use your hands to apply the pressure to correct the bend. Continually sight down the shaft from both ends to determine your progress. It will probably take several minutes to completely straighten the shaft. When you

Heat can also be used to help straighten the shafts. Apply grease, such as cooking oil, shortening, or lard to the shaft.

think the shaft is straight, lay it out on a smooth, flat surface and roll it across the surface to check. It should roll evenly. If it doesn't roll evenly, continue heating and bending until it rolls smoothly.

Heat over a small fire, turning to heat the shaft evenly. Do not allow it to scorch or burn.

Tie the shoots up in bundles of about a dozen shafts each. Use lengths of sturdy nylon string spaced about 3 inches apart to hold the shafts tightly together and as straight as possible. One method of dry-

Use barbeque gloves or hot pads to bend the shafts straight.

Roll the straightened shaft on a smooth flat surface to test for straightness.

Tie the straightened shafts in bundles and place in a warm, dry place to cure.

ing them straight is to insert a steel rod or a ¾-inch straight wood dowel into the bundle and tie the shoots tightly to it. Make sure all shoots are arranged straight in the bundle. Place in a warm, dry, but not hot, location. Do not place them in the sun, which will dry them out too quickly and may cause them to twist and warp. Allow the shafts to dry and cure for about two months.

DEBARKING AND SIZING

Remove the shafts from the bundle and, using a sharp knife, peel off all the bark. Once the bark is removed, you're ready to cut the

After the shafts have cured, remove from the bundle and peel off the bark with a sharp knife.

shafts down to a rough finished size. In most instances, the shaft should be of the same diameter from end to end, but you may also wish to create a Plains tribes–style arrow with a somewhat enlarged nock end. Wooden blunts, or arrows without stone or metal points, were also extremely common. In this case, the shafts were enlarged on the ends, creating the blunt ends as part of the shaft. If creating wooden blunts, the shaft should be sized only to about 3 inches from the proposed blunt end. These types of arrow shafts were more commonly made of "splits."

The Native American arrows were originally worked with sharp-edged flint scraping tools. If you're a purist, you may wish to make some scrapers as described in Section I and use them to shape the arrows. The arrows can also be rough-sized with a sharp woodworking knife, small drawknife, or small block plane. Do not attempt to bring the shaft down to a completed, finished size. Instead, merely smooth off the rough spots, bumps, and slight kinks, and bring the shaft into a fairly consistent round shape.

Once you have the shafts debarked and rough-sized, retie them back into bundles as before, and place in a warm, but not hot, area with plenty of ventilation for the final drying and curing. Most hardwood shoots selected for arrows will dry to a hard, dense wood that will smooth and polish well in about six months.

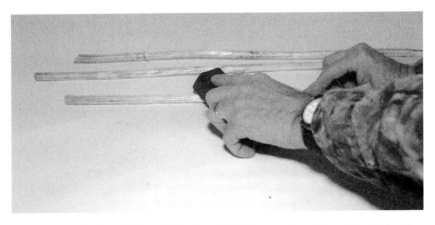

Use a sharp knife, drawknife, or block plane to further smooth and shape the shafts. Then retie in bundles and allow to cure again for about six months.

FINAL SHAPING

The rough-shaping should bring the shaft within 90 percent of the final, finished size. The final shaping finishes the shaft and brings it down to final size. The final shaping also does any re-straightening that may be needed. Again, purists can use primitive stone tools. The arrows can also be final-shaped with a fine woodworking file, a block plane set to a very fine cut, a Stanley Shurform tool, or even rough sandpaper on a sanding block. You will need a sizing tool to make sure the shafts are correctly sized end to end (except for blunts and enlarged nocks) and also that all arrows are approximately the same size. This insures all arrows from a batch shoot in the same manner. The primitive versions of arrow shapers were nothing more than an antler or bone with

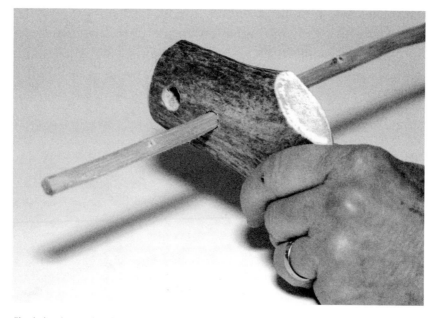

Final shaping and sizing brings the arrows to a "matched" size and shape. Make a sizing tool, a piece of antler with a hole in it the size you wish to make the arrows. As you work the arrows into size and shape, regularly check the diameter with the sizing tool.

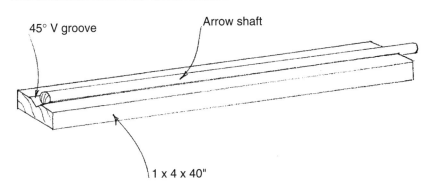

A ¾-inch piece of wood with a shallow groove cut in it can be used to hold the shafts while shaping.

holes in them the desired size of the arrows. The final shapers were, in many instances, the same tools used for occasional straightening of bent arrows. One other tool can also be extremely handy for final shaping of the shafts. A ¾-inch-thick-by-3-inch-wide piece of wood, as long as the arrow shafts and with a groove cut through its center, can be used as a "cradle" to hold the shaft in place and prevent it from rolling and turning while you work the shaft surface smooth.

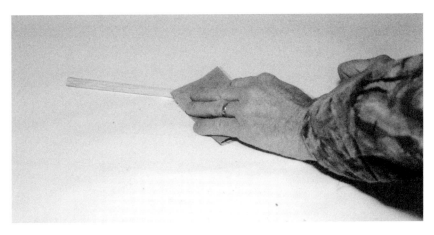

Sandpaper is used for the final shaping. Then use steel wool to polish the shaft.

Take your time as you carefully work the surface of the shafts down to a round, smooth surface, with a consistent shaft diameter throughout. The last-minute finishing should be done with sandpaper wrapped around the shaft and worked back and forth lengthwise. Continually check for the final size with the sizing tool.

Chapter

8

SPLIT SHAFTS AND REED ARROWS

Split shaft arrows can be made from seasoned purchased wood, or you can again obtain the raw materials in the form of green wood cut in the timber, season it, and saw or split it to the rough blank size. The wood you choose is determined mostly by availability. You may be able to cut your own, or you may need to purchase the wood. Split timber shafts are a bit harder to make because the wood has to first be shaped into a round. But, these arrows may also be more stable, especially if from kiln-dried woods.

If you purchase kiln-dried woods you can immediately start making shafts. If you cut your own wood, you'll first have to saw or split the log section into planks or shakes. Large or small diameter logs can be used for obtaining the planks. Heartwood makes the best arrows, so it may take several small logs to obtain good, straight-grained planks. Also, choose a log that doesn't have any knots or other deformities. A portable band-saw mill such as the TimberKing is excellent for sawing the blanks, as is a chain-saw mill. The planks should be at least 1 inch thick, and at least 6

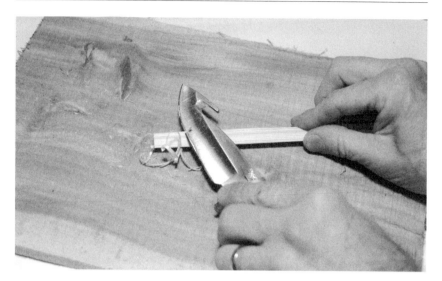

Split shafts were very common. They can be self-arrows or footed arrows, and were also very commonly made into arrows with built-in blunt tips. Splits are basically squares that have their edges rounded.

A portable band-saw mill, such as the TimberKing, can be used to rough-saw blanks used for arrows, as well as bows.

inches longer than the desired arrow length. Once cut, the planks must be cured.

Air-drying is the most common method of curing lumber and it's quite easy. The top of a garage or house attic is the ideal spot. Lay a scrap board across the joists, making sure it is flat and not laid in a bowed position. Then lay ½-inch-thick wood "stickers" across the board and lay a plank down on top of the stickers. Repeat the layers of stickers and planks until all planks

Planks can be home air-dried or kiln-dried.

are laid in place. Place a layer of stickers and a scrap board over the pile. Next, weight the scrap board down with heavy books or a few bricks. Check to make sure the planks are laid straight and not warped. The stickers allow for air circulation around the planks and more even drying. About once a week, turn the boards over and end for end to prevent warping. In approximately two to three months the boards should be air-dried down to about 25 percent moisture content. You're now ready to begin making arrow shafts.

If you don't have a means of sawing, the logs can also be split into "shakes" of about 1 to 2 inches thick. This can be done with a heavy hammer and a couple of wood splitting wedges or, for small saplings, a froe and hammer. Although this method doesn't provide consistently sized blocks to begin with, when split, the blocks tend to follow the grain. These blocks should also be stickered and air-dried in the same fashion as sawed planks.

If you don't have a saw, shakes can be split off log sections to create the blanks.

The cured planks can also be split into strips using a small froe or large chisel.

The next step is to cut the planks or shakes down into a rough-sized arrow blank. This can be done by splitting with a large knife blade and lightweight hammer, tapping on the knife blade. You can also use a froe. A small basket maker's froe from Woodcraft Supply is an excellent tool for the chore. Make the splits about ½ inch thick and then split them again at ½ inch to create blanks of ½-by-½-inch thickness. Most wooden arrows used for hunting are about ⅜ inch thick in diameter and this allows for smoothing and shaping. Hardwood shafts can be slightly smaller in diameter since they're harder. Note: If you're making arrows with carved blunts, you'll need to make the splits big enough for the blunt ends. In most instances, they should be about ¾ inch by ¾ inch.

In case the shakes won't split into straight blanks, you may have to saw them into the sizes needed. But first you'll have to clamp the shake in a wood vise and use a jack plane to create a smooth, flat, beginning surface. Then use a table saw or band saw with a resaw fence to cut the blanks.

Planks that were sawn in the first place are treated in much the same manner. Plane or joint one beginning edge. Then use a table saw, radial arm saw, band saw

The easiest method is to saw the planks into the strips needed for arrows. A table saw or band saw with a resaw fence can be used.

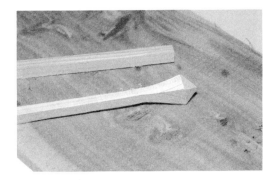

Shown are a standard size shaft and a larger shaft cut with a blunt tip and ready to be shaped.

with resaw fence, or even a portable circular saw with a guide to rip the plank into strips of the proper size. Re-ripping the last cut to create the square can be done with anything but the portable circular saw. You can also use a very sharp ripping handsaw for the chore. If using 1-inch planks that have been home-cured, they should first be planed down to about ½-inch thickness using a planer.

CREATING THE ROUND

You should at this point have a rough square blank ½ by ½ inch in thickness. Lay the blank on a smooth, flat woodworking bench. Use a small hand block plane to further shape and smooth one side. Then turn the smoothed side down and plane the opposite surface. Use a pair of calipers along the length of the shaft to make sure it is planed to the same thickness. A power planer

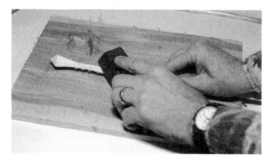

Lay the shaft on a flat, smooth surface and use a small block plane to plane any roughness off the sides.

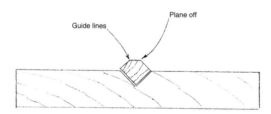

The "shaping" board, with a 45-degree groove, is used to hold the shaft while you plane off one corner. Then turn the shaft and plane off the next corner.

Continue until you have a rough "round" shaft.

makes this chore quick and easy. Repeat the smoothing and planing for the other two sides. The next step is to turn the blank into a round and this is simpler than you might think. You will need a plank as long as the arrow shaft blanks. Cut a shallow, 45-degree groove through the center and the length of the plank. This can be done with a router and a 45-degree bit, or simply with a hand chisel and a little time. Lay the squared "dowel" in the groove and use the block plane set to an extremely fine cut to remove the "corner." Turn the dowel and repeat for the other corners. This will result in an octagon shape. Continue turning and planing until you create a round dowel. You will also need a sizing tool and this can be nothing more than a ¾-inch thick block of wood with a ⅜-inch diameter hole bored in it. As you shape the dowel into a round, use the sizing gauge to final-shape down to the correct diameter.

Use a sizing tool to continue checking the size.

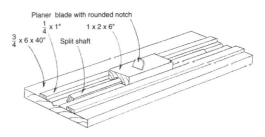

A "rounding" plane jig can be created if you intend to do a lot of arrows.

If you intend to make a number of arrows, you may wish to make up a "rounding" plane jig. This consists of a handmade plane with a hand-ground blade one-half the diameter of the desired shaft. The plane is guided over the arrow blank with guides placed on the holding plank.

CREATING BLUNTS

A small spokeshave or drawknife is the best tool for cutting shafts down to the size needed from blunt tips, and also to shape the blunt tips. A sharp carving knife can also be used to shape the

Blunts are created by first "sizing" the shaft down from the larger blunt tip to the finished shaft size. Use a drawknife, spokeshave, or sharp knife for the initial shaping. A band saw can also be used to "rough cut" the blank to the blunt shape.

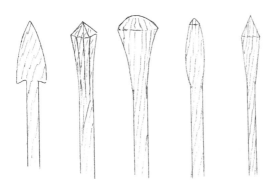

Several different shapes were utilized for the tips of the blunt.

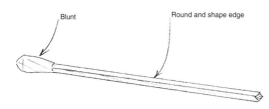

Once the blunts have been shaped, the remainder of the arrow is finished.

tips, or you can use a band saw. In many instances, Native American tips were created with a fluted outside. Once the blunt ends have been shaped, the remainder of the shaft is rounded in the manner described earlier.

RAISED NOCKS

Some tribes also utilized raised nocks to allow for better two-finger pinch gripping of the arrow. These enlarged diameters must also be allowed for in shaping the shaft. Shape the raised nock diameters first, and then finish shaping and sizing the rest of the shaft.

GROOVED ARROWS

Many tribes also grooved their arrows.

These grooves may have served several purposes. They were decorative and they lightened the shaft, but still allowed for strength. Some say they were "blood grooves." Native American weapons builder and author Jim Hamm suggests the grooves may also help keep the arrow straight after they have been heated and straightened.

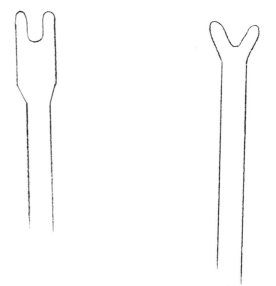

Raised nocks were often common as well. These also require a somewhat larger shaft size then the final size. Shape the nocks first, and then finish the shafts.

Grooving is fairly simple with a handmade grooving tool. It consists of an L-shaped piece of wood with a notch cut in it and a sharp point, such as a nail filed sharp and fastened in the center of the notch. The tool is pulled along the

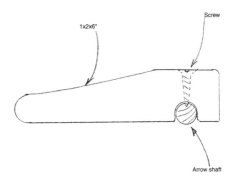

Grooves were also often cut into arrows. A hand-grooving tool makes this chore easy.

length of the arrow to create the groove. The arrow may have three or four grooves cut in it depending on your choice.

As you can see, making arrows can become quite personal.

Once the arrow shaft is made into a round, it is sanded with progressively finer grits of sandpaper.

Tight fit over bowstring

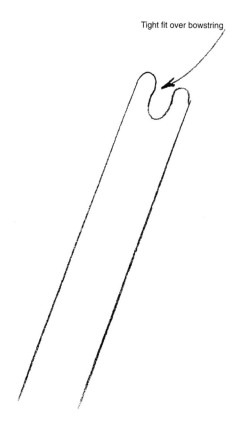

The most common nock is a notch cut in the end of the shaft. The nock must be cut to the correct size in order to hold the arrow on the string.

FINISHING

Once the arrow is shaped into the round, it is finish-smoothed with progressively finer grits of sandpaper. Continually check for size and roundness as you sand and smooth the shaft. Bumps and irregularities can be removed by rolling the shaft on a smooth flat surface and at the same time using a powered finishing pad sander.

CREATING NOCKS

As we mentioned, some arrows utilized raised or enlarged diameter nocks. Whether the nock is raised or the same diameter, the next step is to cut off the shaft above any splits or irregularities. In most instances, you will simply be cutting a notch in the end of the shaft to hold the bowstring. It is extremely important that the notch be cut perpendicular to the edge grain of the shaft. This allows the grain layers of the arrow to be at a 90-degree angle to the bowstring. Carefully examine the shaft to determine the grain layers.

The nock can be initially cut using a small, fine-toothed backsaw. Mark the dimensions of the nock and with the shaft lightly clamped in a padded woodworking vise, saw each side first, and then saw out the middle section to

Make the initial cuts using a fine-toothed backsaw.

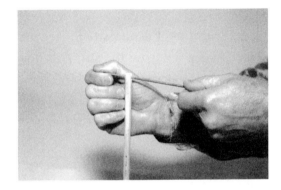

Then use a small flat file to remove the material between the saw cuts.

Sand the nock.

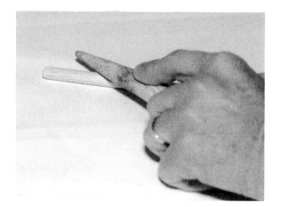

The final step is to burnish the shaft with a piece of antler.

complete the notch. Cut the notch somewhat undersized, and then use a gunsmith's small flat file to complete the inside dimensions. It is extremely important for the nock to properly fit your bowstring. It should snap onto the string and stay in place. If the nock is too small, however, it may break when the arrow is snapped from the string. If it is too large, the arrow won't stay in place. String up your bow and carefully file, sand, and fit the nock until it fits properly. Once you have the notch cut correctly, you can then shape, round, and smooth the remainder of the nock portion.

The final step is to burnish the entire shaft with a hard smooth stone or antler section.

REED ARROWS

Reeds and cane were used for arrow shafts because they were lightweight, yet sturdy, and easy to form into arrows. With their light weight they're like today's hollow aluminum or composite arrows—they're faster than comparable solid wood shafts. As with shoot arrows, it's extremely important to select good raw materials. The reeds should

Reed arrows are extremely lightweight, but strong. They are also heated and bent to straighten as necessary. Inserts are glued in the reed arrows to hold solid wood nocks and points or point holders.

be of the same approximate size since you can't do a lot to change their diameter and/or shape. They should also be as straight as you can get them, with no angular joints. You will have a lot of waste on the ends of the reeds so they should be at last 18 to 20 inches longer than your desired shaft length. Reeds are tapered so the beginning portion of the shaft should be at least 7/16 to 1/2 inch on the largest end. This will usually result in an arrow with a 3/8-inch diameter on the smaller end. There is a lot more waste involved in making reed arrows than shoot arrows; you should acquire about three times as many reeds as you think you'll need arrows. Pull off the leaves and place the reeds in a dry, shady place to air cure for a month or so.

The same heat and bending treatment to straighten the shaft that is used for shoot arrows is used for reed arrows. Because the reeds are hollow, they tend to break if too much pressure is applied. Go very slowly and gently.

Once you have all the shafts straightened, cut a shaft to the correct length. Use this shaft to match the lengths and diameters for the remaining reeds, shifting the shaft up or down on the reed length to get the best match. Smooth and polish the shafts. Because reed arrows are hollow, they are not very strong at the ends and will break easily if the ends strike a solid object. Nocks and solid point holders or solid blunt points must be cut and inserted into the ends of the reed arrows. Allow for this extra length when cutting the reeds. These inserts are held in place with melted pitch or animal hide glue and sinew wrappings.

Chapter
9

PAINTING, FINISHING, AND FLETCHING

Decoration as well as fletching distinguished the Native American individual's arrows, and this decoration still distinguishes arrows today. Painted bands around the arrow, now called "cresting," were popular with Native Americans. Full painted shafts were also common and other designs such as spirals or dots were often incorporated. Almost any waterproof paint can be used. Bright lacquers, however, do not have the same look as the primitive paints. Non-gloss, flat exterior paints are the best choices. To create an even cresting, build a cradle to hold the arrow. Then turn the arrow in the cradle while holding the paint-laden brush against the turning arrow.

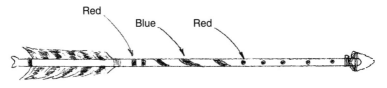

The decoration and the fletching distinguished individual arrows of the Native Americans. Decoration can also distinguish your arrows as well.

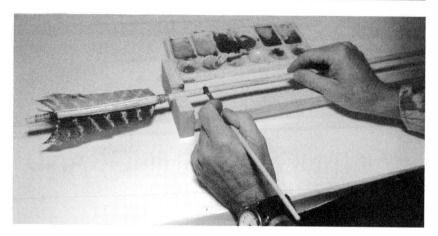

Cresting was a popular method of identifying arrows. A cresting cradle makes this chore easy.

After applying any decoration, the arrow shaft must be finished to protect the decoration as well as the shaft. The modern method is to dip the arrow shafts in a finish using a dipping tube.

Hand-rubbed linseed oil provides the final finish. Use several coats, well rubbed into the wood.

You can make a dipping tube quite easily from a piece of 1-inch plastic water supply line with a cap glued on one end. Do not apply a glossy finish—it detracts from the "primitive" appearance. Glossy arrows are also not effective hunting arrows. A hand-rubbed finish on arrows has a mellower, more "aged" appearance. A number of commercial rub-on oil finishes are perfect, including those produced for gunstocks. You can also make up your own from equal parts boiled linseed oil and shellac. Using your fingers rub the entire shaft to coat it well. Then wipe down and remove the excess finish with a soft cloth. Allow the finish to dry, and then apply three to four additional coats, allowing drying time between each coat and rubbing each down to a soft sheen.

FLETCHINGS

Fletchings also served as "identifiers" but they also had the same purpose as today's fletchings—to stabilize the shaft in flight. Styles of fletchings varied a great deal. Some were large, some were small, and some were attached at both ends with sinew. Some were attached the full length of the fletching with glue as well as sinew, and some were attached only at their front edges. Some Native American arrows were even used without fletchings. The number and spacing of the fletchings also varied. Two and three fletchings were common and these were quite often cut or shaped. Sometimes a single or perhaps two small feathers

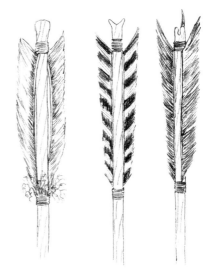

Native American fletchings varied in size, style, and the types of feathers used.

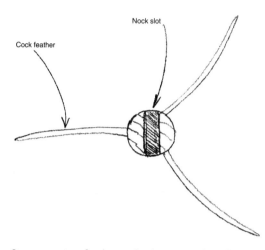

Some were two-feather and others were three-feather fletchings. If three-feather, the fletchings are spaced 120 degrees apart. A cock feather is positioned at 90 degrees to the string.

Native fletching materials include wild turkey and goose wing feathers. Make sure you use feathers from the same wing side for each arrow.

were used whole, simply tied on their fronts as fletchings. The Native Americans used the feathers that were available locally for their fletchings, including buzzard, eagle, hawk, owl, turkey, goose, and even woodpecker and guinea fowl. You can purchase commercial fletching feathers trimmed or untrimmed. If you prefer to create your own, the most common materials for fletching arrows today are wild turkey and Canada or snow goose wing feathers. If you're a hunter, these feathers are readily available and plentiful. If you're not a hunter, you can perhaps barter for them with a hunter.

Determine whether you will utilize two or three fletchings, the latter number being the most common. Also, decide if you are going to install the fletchings straight on the shaft, or in a spiral. Straight fletchings were the most common.

The next step is to determine if you are going to install the fletchings primitive style or with modern methods and materials. The first is slow going at best, but very satisfying. Sinew and hide glue and/or pitch were used to anchor the fletchings in place. First, select a number of feathers of the same approximate size. Always use feathers from the same wing on a fletching, for instance the right or left wing. You can, however, use the different sides on other arrows. Split the feather full length

Rough-cut the fletchings to size, leaving short ends of the base for fastening in place.

Mark locations of the fletchings on the shaft, then position the cock feather in place, making sure it aligns correctly with the nock. Make a couple of wraps of sinew soaked in hide glue around the rear end of the fletching.

with a sharp knife. Then scrape and sand the base of the split feather so it is smooth and even with no bumps, cups, or ridges.

If installing three fletchings, the fletchings are normally fastened in place 120 degrees apart. One feather of a different color than the other two is called a "cock feather," and is set in place at right angles to the nock and bowstring. Precut the fletchings to a rough shape and size and leave the short ends of the "base" on each for fastening with sinew. Using a sharp pencil, mark the locations on the shaft for all the fletchings. Soak a bit of sinew in warm hide glue. Position the cock feather in place and make a couple of wraps of the sinew around the rear end of the fletching. Position another fletching in place and double wrap around the rear end of that as well. Then repeat these steps attaching the rear end of the third feather. Finally, make several wraps around the rear of all the feathers with the hide-glue-soaked sinew. You won't need to tie the sinew. As the sinew dries and the glue sets, the sinew will tighten and hold the fletchings in place.

To complete, lift the front end of one fletching and apply hide glue to the base of the fletching. Position the length of the fletching over the pencil mark. Make a double wrap of the sinew over the front end and repeat these steps for the other two fletchings. Wipe off excess glue and allow the shaft to dry. Granted, this is slow going and messy. Once dry, the fletchings should be

Add another fletching and wrap the sinew thread around the rear end. Then repeat for the third fletching and make several wraps around the end of all three fletchings.

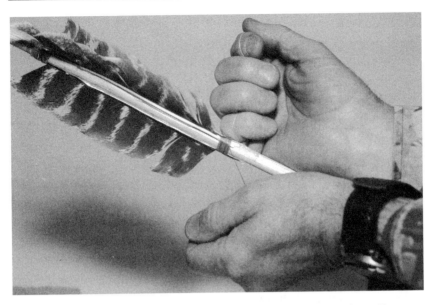

Lift the front end of a fletching and apply a bit of hide glue under the base. Then wrap glue-soaked sinew around the front protrusion of the base. Repeat the steps for the other two fletchings. Wrap around the front bases of all fletchings and allow the glue to dry.

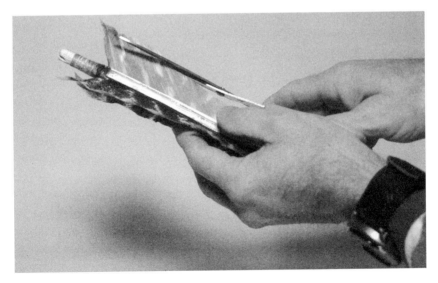

Trim the fletchings to their final sizes.

trimmed to the same approximate size and shape. A sharp knife or scissors can be used for the chore.

A two-feather fletch is done in the same manner, except both fletchings are positioned parallel to the nock or bowstring. Incidentally, the Native Americans often fastened only the ends of the fletchings, leaving the center portion of the fletchings loose.

Of course, you can speed up the chore quite easily by using modern-day materials and methods. The quills can be ground off the feather bases quickly and easily with powered sanders. Fletching jigs precisely position the feathers in place and modern-day fletching glues make the chore much faster and less messy. You can even use electric trimmers to assure that all fletchings are cut to the same size and shape.

Chapter

10

POINTS

Section I dealt with stone and glass points, which are thought of as the most common arrow points, but wooden blunt points were also extremely popular. Wooden blunts were easy to make, less costly to lose, and very effective on small game and

Before adding points, determine the total shaft length needed. One method is to place the nock against your chest and reach out with both hands. Add 1 to 1½ inches to tie on the point.

birds. For the most part, the wooden blunts were cut from the shaft blank on split shaft arrows.

Other point materials included sharpened bone and antler tips. These were made with holes in their bases and the shafts were inserted and glued in place. When it became available, steel was also formed into points and used on arrows.

The first step is to determine the total shaft length needed, or the draw length. Place the arrow nock against the point of your chest, then reach out with both hands, and touch the shaft with your fingertips. That is the arrow length needed, plus the addition of the point. If the point is to be a "tie-on" point, add 1 to 1½ inches to the length. Cut the shaft to the correct length and then cut a notch in the shaft end to receive the point.

Stone points can be hafted in two methods, depending on the point design. The point may not have notches cut in it or

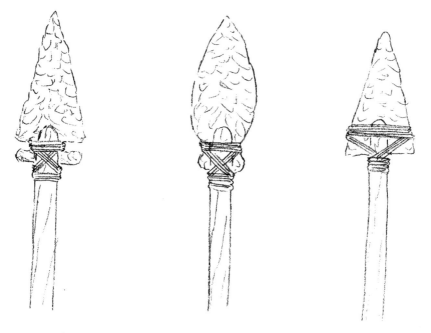

Points may be secured in several ways, depending on the type of point.

Pitch can be used to "glue" the point in place. Then wrap with sinew soaked in warm hide glue.

the notches may be cut in the base or the sides. The points are inserted into a notch cut in the end of the shaft. They are secured with warm hide glue and sinew wrappings. Marty Horn likes to use natural pitch from cedar or pine trees as the "glue." The sinew can be soaked in a bit of warm hide glue before applying. Before the glue and sinew sets up, spin the arrow and sight down the shaft to assure the point is aligned with the arrow shaft.

Metal points can be made of old saw blades, ground to shape and sharpened. They are held in place in the same basic manner.

Before the glue sets up, sight down the shaft and make sure the point aligns with the shaft.

Part III

Bows

Bows and arrows provide much of the mystique of the Native American people. With a couple of pieces of wood, a hand-shaped string, and a piece of rock, these skilled hunters and warriors were able to kill small game and big game (including very dangerous big game), as well as their enemies. The bows ranged from the very crude to sophisticated two-piece and backed bows. Bows and arrows, however, were relative new-comers to the Americas. Bows and arrows have been in use in Europe since 7000 B.C., but evidence shows they had only been used in the New World about a thousand years prior to 1492. Construction varied from region to region. Re-creating these very effective "primitive" bows has become increasingly popular. The chore is challenging, yet fun and instructive. And, you can end up with a bow that is comparable to any of today's similar longbows, and even some recurves. The regional tribes created a wide variety of designs and shapes, with some common factors. Bows were basically of three designs: "self-bows" or those made of one piece of wood; reinforced bows, utilizing sinew or horn pieces to back the wood; or composition bows using a variety of parts and materials. If you are interested in creating your own copy of Native American archery equipment, research the designs from your own region. Many local museums display examples. You can also decide what your main objective is in building the bow, and utilize a design to match your objective. For instance, if you plan to hunt deer-sized animals with the bow, it should have at least a 45-pound pull.

Chapter

11

BOW-BUILDING MATERIALS

The Native Americans were great at using what was available, and this included woods used for making bows. Purists will do the same, and use woods they can acquire from local timber lots. Make sure you have permission to cut any trees for the bow woods. In theory, almost any wood can be used to make a bow. Some, however, are much more durable and effective as woods for bow building. Some of the most common bow woods included: the white woods; ash, elm, hickory, maple, and black locust. Others include: juniper, mulberry, black gum, walnut, maple, and one of the most popular, Osage orange, or bois d'arc. Other, less popular, woods included: cypress, pine, sassafras, and birch.

The different species have unique characteristics, but all share features important to a bow. The first is durability, the second is resiliency, and the third is light weight. Yew has traditionally been one of the most common woods used for bow building, both in Europe and in America. It's extremely bendable, yet sturdy and lightweight. The latter is why it has been a popular wood for longbows. Yew, however, is not readily available locally to many bowyers. Hickory was one of the most popular bow woods and with good reason. Hickory is extremely resilient, takes

Many woods can be used to create Native American–style bows. Hickory and Osage orange were favorites.

stretching quite easily on the back of the bow, and withstands compression on the belly without undue cell damage. It is also easily worked and fairly commonly found. One of the most popular woods was Osage orange, sometimes called hedge or "horse apple." Osage orange is extremely hard, durable, and resilient. It will take repeated bending and last a long time. It is also fairly common in many parts of the country. In fact, it grows readily from a cut stump, producing straight bow staves fairly quickly. If you find the right piece, it works quite easily. If you attempt the wrong piece, however, you'll have lots of frustrations.

BOLT SELECTION

Which brings up the next factor: the workability of the wood piece selected. Take your time in selecting and cutting the wood bolt you will be using for staves. Bow staves may be split from a bolt or length of log, or they may be sawn. If the wood is to be split, the ease with which the wood splits is also important. Elm is the toughest, hickory next, with Osage orange somewhat easier

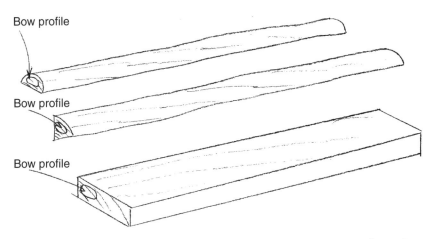

Bows can be made from saplings, split in half; logs split into quarters or smaller; or from planks. The most important factor is to choose a piece of wood as straight as possible and with straight grain.

Knots caused by timber growth can also be extremely hard to work around and should be avoided if possible.

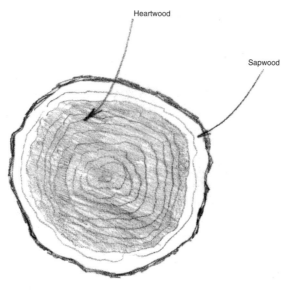

Heartwood

Sapwood

Osage orange

For the most part, bows should be cut from heartwood, not the sapwood.

than hickory. Logs that are to be split should be extremely straight grained. One clue is the bark. If the bark is straight up and down the log, the grain is probably fairly straight. A log with bark spiraling around it will probably split and twist. Sawn logs are not as much a problem, but again a straight-grained log is easier to work with in the long run. The log should also be as straight as possible. It's usually impossible to find an absolutely straight log, and the stave will probably need to be bent somewhat to straighten it before the bow is finished. The straighter the blank, however, the easier the bow-making chore. Needless to say, the stave should be knot free. This is especially so with split blanks and for the first-time bow maker. After you gain experience you'll learn to work around small "pin knots," such as those commonly found in Osage orange, and simply let them add "character" to the bow.

The next factor is size. You may have to do with what you can find. Bows should be constructed using only the heartwood, not the outer sapwood layer. Smaller sapling-sized logs may not have enough heartwood to create certain types of bows. Larger logs, of course, will require more initial effort in sawing and/or

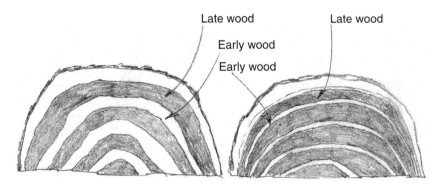

Wood consists of yearly rings with spring or early wood and summer or late wood alternating. The best bow blanks have larger summer wood sections. The wood is denser and less likely to break under stress.

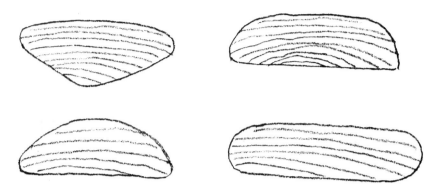

Shown are end-view bow layouts.

splitting. Depending on the species, logs from 6 to 8 inches are good choices with those up to 10 to 12 inches providing some of the best staves. Unfortunately, some of the important facets of a good bow bolt are not evident until the log has been cut, revealing the amount of heartwood and sapwood and the makeup of the growth rings. It is also important to understand the difference between spring wood and summer wood. Each year's growth ring is made up of first a spring wood, and then a summer wood. The spring woods are the lighter-colored layers of the ring, the summer wood the darker. The spring-wood portions of the rings are formed when the sap first begins to rise, and they are more porous, spongy, and softer. Summer woods are less porous and denser. A bolt that has large spring-wood sections as compared to small summer-wood sections will be more brittle and prone to break. A tree section showing larger summer-wood sections will be more durable and have greater resilience.

GREEN OR CURED

You can actually make a bow right from a sapling or bolt, shaping it to suit and then shooting it. Making a green bow is quite easy because the wood works fairly easily. And, as the bow cures, it may pick up more poundage. A green bow, however, does have one major problem. It tends to "follow the arrow." In other words, the bow bends forward toward the arrow after the release, creating a softer and slower shooting bow. For the most part, you're better off cutting the bolt into a stave or staves and curing the staves for about a year.

Most woodworkers prefer to cut wood in the dead of winter when the "sap is down." With less water in the cells, this provides wood that cures more consistently. The bolt should be cut at least 2 feet longer than the desired bow length. This allows for cutting off the inevitable end cracks after the stave cures. As soon as the bolt has been cut, coat both ends with paraffin, varnish, or woodworker's glue. Make sure the entire surface is well coated and sealed.

At this point bowyers differ. Some prefer to split the bolt into staves and allow the individual staves to cure. Others prefer to leave the bolt whole and cure it, and then split it into staves after curing. Both methods have their advantages and disadvantages.

A bow can be made from a green bolt, but the best method is to cut the log or sapling into rough size staves and cure them for about a year.

Splitting the bolts allows the staves to cure faster, and reveals the shape and number of staves you'll get from the bolt. It will normally take at least a year for a stave to air cure down to the minimum 25-percent moisture content. The main disadvantage is the staves may twist and warp while curing. If you allow the bolt to cure in the round, it will take up to two to four years to cure. By that time, natural cracks will have begun in the ends and you can use these as natural "highways" to more easily split the log with the grain. The best method is actually a combination of both methods. Allow the bolt to dry for a couple of months. By that time, minute cracks will appear as guidelines. Then split into staves and allow the staves to cure for another ten to twelve months. Regardless of the method used, the bark should be removed before the curing process because it attracts and harbors borers that can damage some woods. If the bolt has been split into staves, the sapwood should also be removed since the sapwood of some species also attracts insects.

CURING

Air-drying is a traditional method of curing wood. Air-dried wood has been used for the finest furniture and cabinetry in the world, as well as for fine bows. Air-drying does take time. In fact, the longer you can leave the stave or bolt, the drier—up to a certain extent. Most woods won't dry down below 10 percent without some sort of curing process. Two years is about the minimum, with four years and longer even better, especially with bolts. The best curing area is a warm, but not hot, dry, but not sunny, place with good circulation. The ideal spot I've found is the hayloft of an old barn. Unfortunately, these days, haylofts are rather scarce. Overhead in a garage, shop, and a well-ventilated attic are other good choices. The idea is to allow the moisture to escape slowly and the heat and air to cure the wood.

The staves can also be rough-shaped down to a single growth ring on the back and allowed to cure for about six months.

Bows can also be made from sawn planks. The planks can be sawn with a portable bandsaw mill such as the TimberKing shown. The planks should then be sawn into 2-by-2-inch blanks and air-dried.

97

It's a bit tricky. Too much heat and the bolt or stave may split further or dry too quickly.

The alternative is to have the wood kiln-dried. The small volume you will be offering, however, does not lend itself to this approach unless you know a local kiln operator. If you're really interested in kiln-drying, however, plenty of information is available on building your own. A number of small kiln designs are available on the Web from the Department of Forest Products, Virginia Polytechnic Institute, and State University Extensions. A good deal of this information is linked through www.woodweb.com.

Some bowyers like to rough-shape the stave, with the back down to a single growth ring, and then allow the stave to cure. This will bring curing time down to about six months. But, the stave may warp or twist; it's one of those chances you simply have to take.

SAWN PLANKS

An alternative to splitting is to saw large logs into 2-inch planks. These planks can then be shaped or resawn into bow blanks or staves. This allows you to follow a single growth ring in order to produce the strongest possible bow. A portable band-saw mill, such as the TimberKing, is perfect for this chore. These planks can be air-dried, which will take several years, or the planks can be sawn into 2-by-2-inch blanks. You can even rough-shape them into staves and allow them to air-dry. The green planks can also be kiln-dried, which takes only a few months to produce stable, dried wood. One very important tool if you do decide to kiln-dry, or even air-dry planks, is a moisture meter. Available from sources such as Woodworker's Supply or Lee Valley, they indicate the amount of moisture in the dried wood. For most

Bow blanks can also be freehand sawn from split bolts using a table saw. For safety, use a push stick and eye protection.

woods, the ideal moisture content for bow blanks ranges between 8 and 10 percent.

PURCHASING

Bow staves or blanks can also be purchased. Kiln-dried planks that can be cut into staves can also be purchased. When purchasing staves use the same care in selecting the stave as when selecting a tree to cut the staves from. The stave should be relatively straight, free of knots, and large enough to cut away any possible defects. If possible, ask for a heavy or "double" stave. This will allow you greater leeway in placing the bow in the blank. Also examine it for bug holes. Many species of wood will have insect damage. If this occurs in the sapwood, for the most part, they won't be as much of a problem.

Of course, you can also purchase kiln-dried wood planks and cut staves from them. You probably won't, however, be able to acquire some species in planks, for instance, bois d'arc. Ash, maple, and hickory may be available. One advantage of purchasing planks is you can cut several staves from a wide plank and immediately start making a bow, rather than cutting a tree and waiting for the wood to cure.

Chapter

12

SPLITTING AND/OR
ROUGH-SAWING THE STAVE

If you begin with a bolt or log, it must be split or sawn to create
the stave. Splitting the bolt or log is the traditional method.

*Splitting is the typical method of acquiring a bow stave from a bolt. Use an axe or froe to
start a crack in the smaller end of the bolt or log.*

SPLITTING

Some woods split fairly easily, resulting in a nice, straight or fairly straight stave. Others may provide a straight stave, but are extremely hard to split. The hardest wood to split is elm—you'll probably end up learning a few choice words if you attempt it. In most instances, the log is first halved, then quartered, and then staves split from the quarters. You may prefer to saw the staves from the quarters.

The technique of splitting is fairly simple. I've split logs for everything from split-rail fences to wooden shakes, as well as for bow staves. In most instances, a natural crack will occur in the ends of the log. Place a sharp-edged wedge, hatchet, or froe in the crack. Hammer the device into the crack using a maul or heavy ball-peen hammer. Drive the device about three-quarters of the way into the crack, or until you can position a second wedge into

Drive a wedge into the starting crack.

Once a crack develops back from the first wedge, drive another wedge in place until the first wedge is loosened.

Continue leap-frogging the wedges until the log is split.

the started crack and about a foot down the log. As you tap the second wedge in place, the first will loosen. Remove the first wedge and leapfrog it over the second wedge. Continue driving the wedges until the log splits. If you're lucky, the split will provide two approximately half logs of a fairly straight nature. More often, however, the split will result in one end of the split log being thicker than the other, as the split follows the natural grain. An alternative method is to drive a wedge in the middle of the log and split toward both ends. This sometimes results in a more consistent-sized split. In most instances, you will have to use a sharp axe or hatchet to separate some of the splinters that often run out of the grain and continue to hold the split pieces together.

If you're working with a small sapling you may now have one or two split pieces suitable for roughing into a stave. With a larger log you'll need to quarter the halves. On fairly large logs the quarters are also split.

SAWING

You can also saw the logs into planks and then into staves. These days a number of small, one-man, portable band-saw mills make

Or the log can be sawn into planks.

the chore easy. The model I've used is a TimberKing 2400. It will easily saw logs in the 8- to 10-inch diameter into 2-inch thick planks. Because the TimberKing 2400 uses a thin but large band saw, the resulting plank surfaces are relatively smooth. These band-saw mills have also become quite popular as "extra-income" tools. Check locally to find an operator near you to do the chore as well.

At this point, the log may or may not need to be cured as described in Chapter 1.

ROUGH-SHAPING STAVES

By now you should have decided what style and size bow you are going to make. The blank is now cut down to the widest width and thickest portion. These measurements should typically be 2 by 2 inches. This can be done in one of two ways, using a drawknife (or even with a hand hatchet) or with a band saw. The following chapters illustrate creating different bow styles and sizes.

Rough-shape the blank to 2-by-2-inch size and about a foot longer than the final length desired.

Chapter
13

CREATING SELF-BOWS

S elf-bows refer to bows made of one piece of wood without backing of any kind. Self-bows can be longbows or a shorter version. Longbows of 5 to 6 feet in length were very popular with the Woodland and eastern Native American tribes. Many of these bows were made of hickory or other "white" woods. The prairie

The Native Americans utilized several different bow designs and lengths. The Woodland tribes commonly utilized longer-length bows. These were in much the same design as European "longbows." The Plains tribes utilized shorter, flatter, and wider bows, primarily for use on horseback.

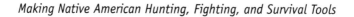

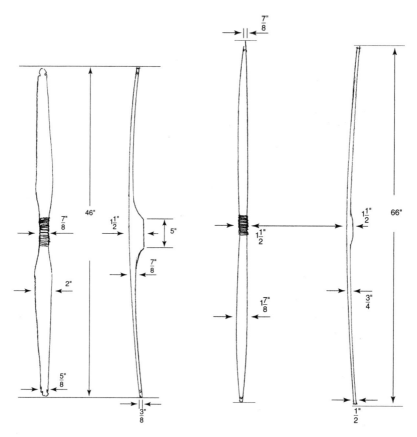

Shown are measurements for typical Woodland longbows and Plains bows.

tribes preferred shorter bows because mounted horsemen often used these bows. Osage orange was a favorite material for these shorter bows.

CREATING A HICKORY LONGBOW

In this method, we illustrate cutting a bow with a band saw. The material can be a split stave, sawn stave, or sawn stave cut from a plank. The first step is to decide the length of the bow. If you want a bow to precisely match your stature, you should measure your draw length. Bows for a draw length of 26 inches should be

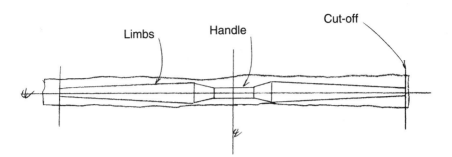

The first step is to lay out the bow on the stave. With the belly of the bow blank facing down, begin with a centerline. Then mark the handle, the length of the limbs, and the tip widths. Next, mark between the handle area and tips to outline the limbs.

around 66 inches; 68 inches would suit a 28-inch draw length; and a 30-inch draw length works well with a 70-inch stave. Native American longbows ran from just over 5 feet up to more than 6 feet in length. Draw weight can vary from just over 45 up to 70 or more pounds, depending on the tillering. The bow we will describe is a typical "D" bow or one resembling a flattened D when strung. Examine the stave for knots or any other potential problems and lay out the bow on the stave to avoid as many knots or problems as possible. For instance, on an 8-foot stave you can shift the bow layout up and down on the stave quite a distance if necessary. The following bow layout is an example of a commonly used pattern. You may wish to alter the layout to suit yourself. If it hasn't already been done, remove any bark and sapwood from the stave with a drawknife, stripping down to a single layer of heartwood.

The first layout step is to mark across the stave for the center of the bow. If the stave has a slight natural bend on one end, choose that as the upper limb. Mark the upper and lower ends of the handle and then mark the ends of the upper and lower limbs. Finally, use a straight edge to mark a centerline the length of the back of the bow. Measure and locate the midpoints of the limbs

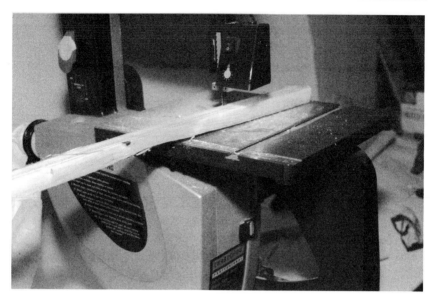

With the belly of the bow down, saw the rough outline of the bow using a band saw or saber saw. Or you can rough-shape with a hatchet, drawknife, or sharp knife.

and lay out the bow on the front surface. Make sure your edge side is flat and smooth. Lay out a rough size for the thickness of the bow, including the handle, if you are adding one. Many Native American longbows were made without a distinctive handle area; some had a thickened area for the handle.

With the flat side down, cut off any excess from the back. Do not follow the contour of the handle, but cut to the thickest portion. Turn the stave back over onto the flat cut portion and use the band saw to cut the outline marked on the top or the front of the stave face. At this point, you have a rough outline seen from the front of the bow. You can also use a hatchet, drawknife, woodworking rasp, or other tools to rough-shape the stave. Lightly round all front edges and smooth the front face, but do not cut into the first revealed ring established at first. Now mark the thickness of the stave on both upper and lower limbs. The thickness tapers

If possible, cut the back of the bow down to a single growth ring using a wood rasp, sander, or drawknife. Then lightly round all the front edges and smooth up the front face.

Turn the stave over on one side and mark the desired tip thickness. Mark approximate thickness at the center of each rib. Use a flexible straight edge to mark between the tip, limb center, and the handle area on each limb.

towards the ends. The profile pattern shown at different locations on the stave is a good guideline, but each bow will be unique and the measurements are simply guidelines. Use a thin piece of wood to connect between the measurements and make a cutting

Again, use a band saw, wood rasp, drawknife, or other tool to cut away the excess wood to create a rough "side-shape" of the stave.

guideline. Make sure you don't overdo the thinning process at this time—you can't put it back. Note if the back of the bow is not straight, but has slight curves in it, and follow the curves to maintain the same thickness desired. Do not cut more thinly at the curved areas. Next, use the band saw again to cut the blank to the desired thickness. You can also lock the blank in a vise and use a rough rasp or drawknife to cut to the desired thickness. If using a drawknife, work from the handle towards each end. If the drawknife tends to dig in and follow the grain, work from the opposite end. At this point, the bow profile should be a somewhat flat or rectangular shape and ready for tillering.

TILLERING

From this point on you can create a beautiful working bow, or destroy a piece of wood. You must work carefully and slowly. Grasp

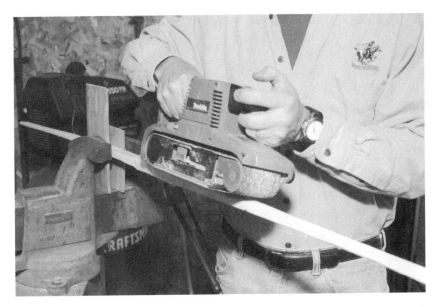

Tillering is slowly removing wood from the belly side of the bow to achieve an even bending of the limbs, and the correct draw weight. Go very carefully. Don't remove too much at a time—you can't put it back. Use a file, sandpaper, drawknife, or spokeshave.

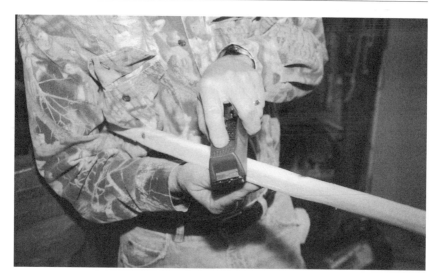

When the bow bends evenly, lightly round the belly edges.

each limb tip with a hand and place your knee against the handle, then bend the bow. Depending on the wood species, you'll probably have a 100- to 150-pound pull bow blank at this time. But you should be able to determine if one limb bends more than the other or if there is an even bend. From this point on, use a file, sandpaper, or scraper to begin slowly removing material from the belly of the bow slightly down past the marked line and to even the bend of the limbs. Once you have removed wood down past the line, re-mark it. This allows you to keep a consistency in slowly removing the wood.

Lightly round the back of the bow edges with sandpaper, and then sand the back as smooth as possible. Start with medium-grit sandpaper and finish with extremely fine grit. Do not, however, sand down through the initial growth ring established on the back of the bow. This smoothing not only adds to the appearance but also removes imperfections that might cause problems later.

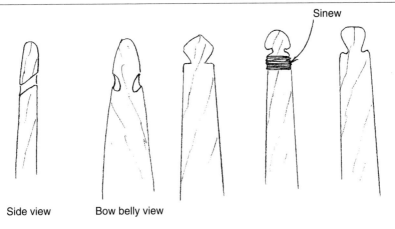

Side view   Bow belly view

Several different styles of nocks were utilized in the bow tips.

At this point you should cut the nocks in the bow tips. Native Americans used several different styles. The easiest to cut and use is the double nock. Cut these with a small round wood file, a sharp knife, or a hand grinder, such as a Dremel tool. Make sure all edges are rounded so they won't cut the string.

If the bow will bend evenly, begin final tillering. Tillering is more art than science. It's very easy to remove too much ma-

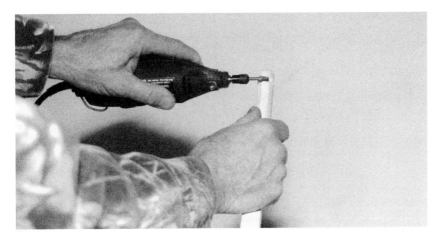

Use a small round file or hand grinder such as a Dremel tool to cut the nocks.

terial. Make a bowstring (see Chapter 1, Section IV) or purchase one long enough so the string height will be about 6 inches from the inside of the handle. Carefully string the bow. If it is still too strong to string, remove a tiny layer of material, again from the belly side of the bow. Try to string the bow again. In most cases, one limb will be stronger than the other. Place the strung bow on a flat smooth surface with graph paper or other paper with marking lines. This will show if one limb bends with more of an arch, illustrating the weakest limb. Carefully rasp and sandpaper wood from the belly of the strongest limb to even up the limbs.

Once you're satisfied with the evenness of the limbs, begin to draw the bow. Bring it back a few inches then slowly return the

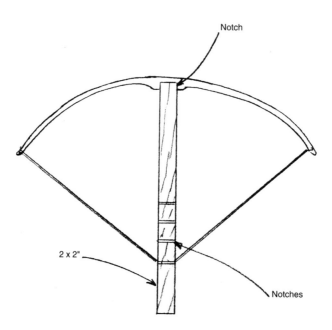

Make a "working" bowstring, then string up the bow and bring it back a few inches. Return the string to the undrawn position, and then repeat several times. If the bow is still too heavy, again lightly remove material from the belly of the bow. A tillering stick can be used to measure the length of the draw and check for evenness.

Lay the drawn bow on a smooth flat surface, such as a floor tile and check that both limbs are drawn evenly. Note the obvious uneven tillering of the bow limbs.

string to the undrawn position. Do this about two dozen times, slowly increasing the draw until you have the bow at the proper draw length. If the bow is too heavy to pull, again lightly remove material evenly from the belly. A tillering stick can be used to measure the draw length. It should have a notch in the top for the bow handle to rest in and marks down one side for draw lengths. A wide foot on the bottom allows it to rest on a bathroom scale and be used to determine the poundage

The handle can be shaped in different ways. Wrapping with rawhide adds a nice touch.

of pull at the same time you're measuring the draw length. This is where patience and the "art" comes in. You're working to create a bow of the proper draw length as well as proper poundage. Continue to refine the bow until you reach the desired draw length and weight. The tillering stick should have a notch cut in it at the desired draw length. It can then be used for final checking to assure both limbs are of equal strength.

Many Native American bows didn't have a distinct handle; others had enlarged handles on the belly with narrowed handles seen from the front or belly. Shape the handle as desired.

FINISHING

Once you're satisfied with the shape of the bow, the final step is to smooth it completely. Use a sharp knife or cabinet scraper, held at right angles to the wood, or steel wool to scrape out the rasps and sanding marks and smooth the belly and sides, rounding the edges very slightly. Many Native American bows had distinctive painted decorations. To apply a painted decoration, use acrylic paints to make up the pattern. Then apply an oil finish to the bow to prevent it from drying out. Traditional finishes were animal

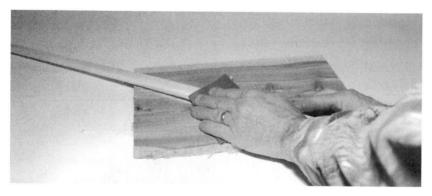

Final sand and polish the bow with a cabinet scraper or decorate the bow with paint. Then apply several coats of boiled linseed oil, rubbing it in thoroughly to add a nice sheen.

fats, such as bear fat. Bacon grease can be used or you can apply boiled linseed oil, wiping it well into the wood and polishing it. Apply several coats of oil.

OSAGE ORANGE FLAT BOW

Another type of popular bow design was the flat bow. These bows were typically shorter, sometimes as short as 4 feet, and were also wider or "flatter" than longbows. The basic steps to create them are the same, except for the difference in layout. In building an Osage orange bow, it's extremely important to begin the back with a single hardwood growth ring. Then cut the bow from that point in the same manner as described for the hickory longbow.

BENDING WOOD

In some instances you will have to bend the stave to straighten it. You can also create a recurve bow, in which case the stave is bent to the shape desired.

RECURVE

By adding a reverse bend to the tips of the limbs of a bow, more energy is stored, producing a flatter shooting and faster bow. The Native Americans were quite adept at producing recurve bows. Making a recurve bow consists of the same basic steps as other bows, with the addition of bending the limbs.

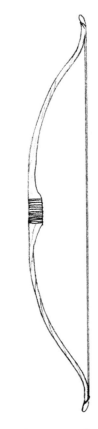

Recurve bows were also popular with the Native Americans, and you can make your own version quite easily.

The ends of the limbs must be heated. A small campfire or charcoal grill can be used.

Whether bending to straighten a stave or to create a re-curve, the basic method is to heat the wood, and then bend it as desired. Either dry heat or steam works, but you must be very careful if you use dry heat. A campfire or even a propane torch wisely applied to an almost finished bow can be used to straighten slight bends. It is, however, quite easy to scorch or burn the wood fibers, as well as to weaken the wood fibers to the point of ruining the bow.

The ancient method was to hold the bow over a bed of coals until it was heated, and then bending it. To try this yourself, first coat the area you want to bend with grease, such as bear fat, and then heat only the tip or portion of the bow to be bent. Keep turn-ing the stave so it heats evenly and watch that the wood doesn't scorch or burn.

Moist or steam heat allows for more precise bending with less chance of causing serious heat damage to the bow. One method of using moist heat is to place the stave or the portion to

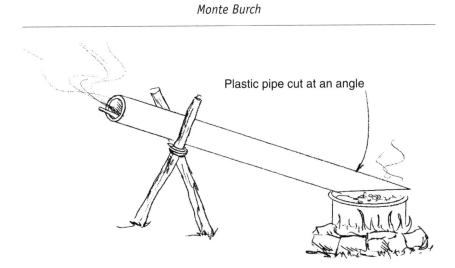

Plastic pipe cut at an angle

Or you can make up a steam-bender from a piece of plastic plumbing pipe and a steam source such as a kettle of water.

be bent into a trough or steel pipe with water. Bring the water to a boil and place the stave or portion to be bent in it. Allow the stave to boil for a couple of minutes, and then try to bend the section. If it won't bend easily, place it back in the water for another minute, and then try again. You can still ruin a stave if overheated, so watch it carefully and check for bendability frequently. Steam heat can also be used to heat the portion to be bent. A steam heater can be created using a section of plastic plumbing pipe with a removable cap on both ends and an opening to a steam source, such as a teakettle, over a campfire or camp stove.

Whichever method is used to heat the wood, as soon as the wood can be bent, it should be bent using potholders or insulated barbeque grill gloves. The area to be bent should be over-bent slightly since the wood will straighten somewhat after it cools. The bent portion should also be held in the bent position until the wood cools completely. A simple bending jig can be made to hold the wood in place. When bending the tips of the stave for recurves, a bending jig also assures both tips will be bent to the same degree.

121

Once the wood is hot, bend carefully, using barbeque mitts. Overbend slightly since the wood will flex back somewhat.

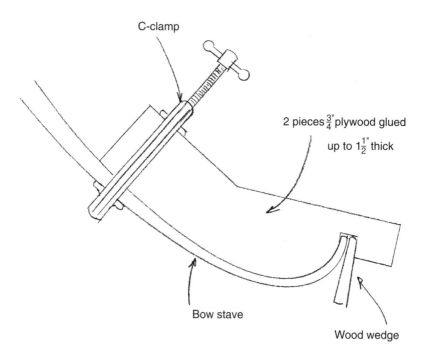

A simple wooden jig can also be used to clamp the bow in place until it "sets."

MAKING A BACKED BOW

The Native Americans also often added a stiffener material to the backs of their bows. This was a common practice with the Plains tribes and their shorter bows. Sinew was used most often, but horn, and even snakeskin were also used. The Eskimos also used backing on their typically short bows as well. Sinew was particularly effective in preventing breakage on the static recurve bows. In fact, a properly designed and made bow backed with sinew is extremely strong and

Many Native American bows were backed with material to make them stronger. Sinew was a common backing. Shown is a sinew-backed bow made by Marty Horn. A snakeskin was applied over the backing.

durable. Making a backed bow does, however, almost double the amount of time and work needed to make a bow. And, for some bowyers, sinew and hide glue may be hard to acquire. If you're an avid deer hunter these days, however, sinew is easy to acquire.

Typically, sinew comes from either the leg or loin of the deer. The leg sinew is actually the Achilles tendon, taken from the lower portion of the leg. A cut is made from the rear hock to the ankle joint between the tendon and the bone and the tendon simply peeled out. You will need eight to ten Achilles

One source of sinew is from the tendon in the lower portion of a deer or elk leg.

Another source of sinew is from the deer loin. Remove the sinew from the loin and then scrape away all flesh.

tendons to make a bow, depending on the size of the tendons and the bow length.

Another type of tendon is found on the outside of the deer loins, just beneath the skin. The tendons are flat, tough membranes. Our family loves venison, especially the tenderloin, and we always trim off the tendons when we process the loins. To remove the membrane, lay the loin on a smooth, flat surface with the membrane on the bottom side. Using a very sharp boning knife, slide the knife between the membrane and the meat. Another method is to remove the sinew before removing the loin from the carcass. Hang the animal by the rear legs and skin it out. Make a cut through the tendon at the hip joint, slice down between it and the meat, and peel it out. Cut the tendon loose from the carcass when you reach the neck area. However close you attempt to trim the tendon, you'll end up with a little meat at-

The sinew must then be air-dried.

tached to it. Spread the membrane out flat on a smooth surface and slice off any meat remaining on it.

The back tendons are more versatile. They can be used for backing bows, making bowstrings, or used as extremely tight "wrapping" thread for fastening points and fletchings in place. It does require a great deal more back tendons for backing a bow, anywhere from eighteen to twenty. You can, however, use a combination of both back and front leg tendons when making a bow.

The tendons can be frozen or dried for later use. The leg and back tendons intended for bow backing are normally dried, while the back tendons, when used for strings and other wrappings, are commonly frozen then used "semi-fresh." The leg tendons dry more quickly if they are "quartered," splitting them lengthwise. Do not allow the tendons to touch while drying, or they may stick together. It's also a good idea to roll or turn them every day or so to allow fresh surfaces to air-dry. All tendons should be stored in a cool, dry place safe from pets and wildlife. Once dried properly, they will take on a translucent appearance and can be stored indefinitely.

Before use, the tendons must be separated into individual threads. This is at best a time-consuming chore. Leg tendons have a tough outer shell. Pound on it to loosen it enough so that it can be peeled away, and then continue to pound on the inner core until it separates into strands. If you're dedicated to tradition, use a large round platform stone and a hammerstone. If using a hammer, utilize a hard metal surface, such as an anvil or even an old railroad tie section. The hammer should be a round-faced metalworking ham-

To use, individual strands or bundles are separated. Pounding on the tendons loosens the fibers. Then pull them apart. Nails in a board can be used as a separator.

mer or maul without sharp edges that can cut through the strands. Wearing safety glasses, pound until the tendons begin to separate, and then use two pairs of locking joint pliers to pull them apart. Continue pounding as needed, and pulling apart the tendon into increasingly smaller strand bundles. Once the tendons are separated into small bundles; you can usually grasp separate strands and pull them apart with your hands or with the pliers. The thinner back tendons are easier to separate. At first, you may have to grasp them with the pliers to start the bundles, but you can then usually separate the strands with your fingers. A nail separator helps. Merely drive No. 4 cement-coated or sheetrock nails through a thin piece of wood. Clamp the wood piece in a vise, nails up, and draw the back tendon across the nail to begin the separations. Once the tendons have been separated into dried strands, place them in a plastic zippered bag and store until needed.

PREPARING THE GLUE

Although modern glues work well, ideally, animal glue should be used to apply the sinew strands to the back of the bow. This can be purchased, or you can make your own from sinew or hide scraps. In making your own, the sinew must be separated or the hide cut into shavings and pulverized. To plump up the materials, soak them for 24 hours in water to which a bit of lye has been added. Use caution in using the lye and lye water. Wear a long-sleeved shirt, long pants, gloves, and eye protection. Then, rinse in clean water and soak in vinegar for a bit to neutralize the acid. Rinse again and you're ready to "cook off" the glue. The materials are placed in a large pot or kettle and covered with water. The glue can be slow-cooked, simmering for up to 24 hours for sinew and 12 hours for hide. Attach a candy thermometer to the side of the pot and bring the water up to 170 to 175 degrees Fahrenheit. Simmer at this temperature, stirring occasionally. Before pouring off, bring the mixture to a boil, which brings the impurities to the surface. Skim off and pour the syruplike glue into flat pans to cool and set up. You can hasten the process by boiling the mixture for a couple of hours or so, or until the liquid turns into a light syruplike thickness. Skim off the impurities and pour. Protect the drying glue from insects and pests. The dried powderlike glue can then be reconstituted anytime you need it by soaking in water. It is then heated before application. Purchased powderhide glues are also available and also reconstituted and heated for use. Titebond liquid hide glue is a genuine hide glue that comes in a ready-to-use liquid form and doesn't require heating. It's also odorless and holds more than 4,000 pounds per square inch.

PREPARING THE BOW

The bow should already be well sanded and smoothed, especially the back and sides. Some woods produce an oil and they should be degreased. Lacquer thinner and a soft cloth can be used to wipe away these oils or you can utilize an old-fashioned method of degreasing with lye water, using a mixture of three parts water to one part lye. Caution: Lye water and lye are extremely caustic and can burn your skin and cause eye damage. Wear a long-sleeved shirt, eye protection and rubber gloves. Brush the solution over the entire bow, then immediately flush off with boiling water. Using the rubber gloves, place the bow in a position so it can be held with the back up.

HEATING THE GLUE

Place the powdered glue in a double boiler and add a bit of hot water to reconstitute the glue. Allow to heat until the glue bulks up and again liquefies. You may need to heat it for several hours to allow it to thicken. Then apply a thinned solution of hide glue to the back and sides of the bow to "size" it. This will help the

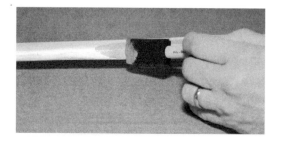

With the powdered glue reconstituted and heated, place the bow in a cradle. Brush a thin coat of glue over the entire back to "size" it.

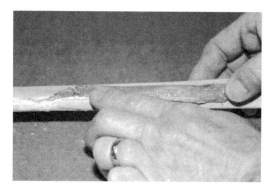

Dip a sinew bundle in the glue and swirl it around to coat it well. Then apply to the back of the bow.

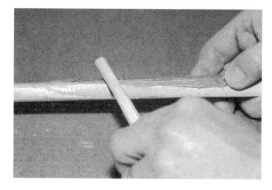

Use a wooden stick with rounded edges, or a piece of antler or bone to smooth the sinew in place.

sinew and additional layers of glue to adhere properly. Place the bow in the "cradle" of blocks on the workbench and allow it to dry thoroughly.

With the glue thoroughly dried, place a large piece of cardboard on the workbench or work surface. Heat the glue in a gluepot or double boiler. The glue should warm enough to spread evenly, but not be too hot to handle, and of the consistency of thin syrup. Spread out enough sinew strand bundles to back the bow properly. Dip a sinew strand bundle in the glue and swirl it around to make sure the entire bundle is well coated. Holding the bundle with the fingers of one hand, strip excess glue away with the fingers of your other hand. The bundle should be well saturated, but not dripping with glue. Lay the sinew bundle onto the back of the bow, with its center in approximately the middle of the bow handle. Use a rounded edge on a piece of wood or bone or an angled piece of antler to smooth the sinew down and press it tightly to the wood surface. This will also somewhat squeegee out the excess glue. Work from the center toward each end, smoothing out the tendons. Hold the bundle in place to make sure it doesn't slide. Then simply continue gluing strips of tendon bundles the length of the bow, butting the ends of the tendons together, but making sure there are no ridges where they join. When you reach the tips of the bow, wrap the tendon bundle around the bow tips. Once this centerline strip has been completed, repeat on both sides, wrapping around to cover at least one-half of the thickness of the bow sides. The bundles should be offset, much like shingles, so there are no cross-the-entire-back areas without tendon bundles.

Once these layers have been applied over the entire back, some bowyers like to add another layer consisting of sinew laid crosswise

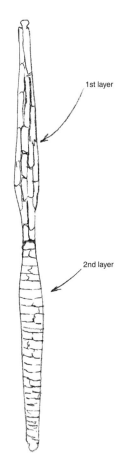

1st layer

2nd layer

Continue gluing sinew in strips to the back, overlapping the joints much like overlapping bricks. Add a second layer going crosswise, and extending over the sides. Then add a third layer over the centerline to build it up. Finally, add a last layer over the entire back. Then coat the entire backing with a thin layer of glue.

over the back. This layer can also be extended down over the sides if desired. The next layer consists of a single centerline layer to build up and round the back of the bow. Then apply a layer lengthwise again, this time with the two sections meeting in the centerline of the bow. For an even stronger bow, add an additional crosswise layer. In essence, you're creating the crosswise layering design of plywood, well known for its strength-to-weight ratio. When you first add all these layers, your once-elegant bow will take on an overblown appearance. But, as the tendons dry, they will shrink. The final step is to coat the entire tendon-backed surface with another coat of hide glue.

CURING

Initial curing should be done with the bow lying on the cradle on the workbench. Curing is best done in a cool, dry environment, but not freezing. The bow also should not be exposed to heat or direct sunlight at this time. Cure for 24 hours. The bow can then be taken outdoors during the daytime and exposed to heat, sunlight, and wind, which will help the bow to cure. Be sure to protect it from chewing rodents, pets, and other animals that may be attracted to the glue. During damp or inclement weather and at night, the bow should be stored indoors. In most instances, it will take about two to three weeks for the bow to cure completely. Do not flex or pull the bow until it has completely cured.

FINISHING

Once the sinew has cured properly, it should be smoothed and finished to match the remainder of the bow. Some bowyers like to cover the sinew with snakeskin. In either case, the rough ridges and bumps must be removed. A cabinet scraper held at right angles does the chore best. A sharp knife can also be used in the same manner. Once the ridges have been removed, the surface can then be sanded with extremely fine sandpaper. When you finish this task, the sinew covering will be smooth, but with tiny ends of sinew sticking up. The final step is to apply a thinned coat of glue to the backing, using your fingers. Allow the surface to dry to a tacky stage, then dip a soft cloth into warm water and polish the surface to a nice sheen.

SNAKESKIN

Snakeskin is a popular backing, used either on a self-bow or a bow with sinew backing. Snakeskin by itself does not add much to the strength of the bow; however, it does make a very attractive covering. A skin, tanned using one of the special snakeskin tanning kits such as that from Rittel's Tanning Supplies, is an excellent choice. This will add some strength to a self-bow and helps keep the back from having minute splintering. Untanned or green snakeskin can also be used. Make sure the skin is completely fleshed before using and install on the bow immediately after skinning. Hide glue or a good waterproof woodworking glue can be used to install the green skin in place. Once the skin has cured

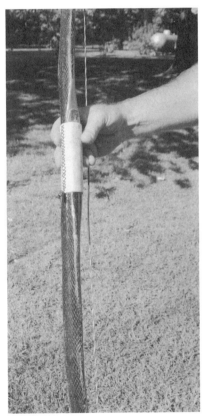

You may wish to add a snakeskin for appearance. You can use either a tanned or green skin, gluing it in place with hide glue. Once dried, scrape the scales off and give a light coat of varnish to protect the skin.

and set to the bow, the scales should be removed. One method is to lightly rub the skin with the end of a kitchen spoon. The scales will pop off easily, leaving the skin and color pattern. After the snakeskin has thoroughly dried, a light coating of varnish can be used to protect it.

COMPOSITE BOWS

Some of the more unusual bows were composite bows, made from the horns of buffalo, antler sections, horns of big horn sheep, and musk ox horns. These "sectional" bows were wrapped with sinew to hold the glued pieces together. Fish glue was often the choice for adhering these bow pieces together.

Part IV

Bowstrings and Quivers

Of course you'll need bowstrings for your bows. Many bowyers prefer to also make their bowstrings of natural, Native American materials. Many primitive weapons aficionados also like to make quivers that are replicas of some of the same styles used by the Native Americans.

Chapter
14

BOWSTRINGS

Bowstrings can be made using all-natural materials in the same manner as the Native Americans made them. They can also be made of modern-day synthetic materials.

NATURAL MATERIAL BOWSTRINGS

Making strings from natural materials is, of course, the hardest and most time-consuming. If you're a purist, however, it's the only

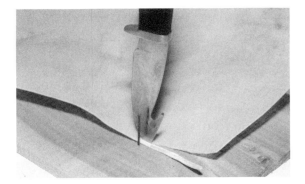

Rawhide was one of the bowstring materials of the Native Americans. To cut long thin lengths, dampen or wet the hide. Make a starting cut, then pull the thin section between a sharp knife and peg driven into a wood block the thickness desired.

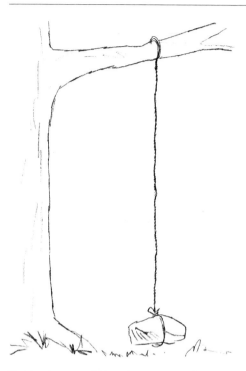

Tie the damp, rawhide strips to an overhead object, such as a tree limb. Tie a heavy weight to the opposite end and turn the weight to twist and stretch the strands. Tie the weight so it won't spin once you get the strands tightly twisted.

way. Natural materials include sinew, gut strings, rawhide, and plant fibers.

RAWHIDE

Rawhide is one of the most primitive, but still effective, materials to use for bowstrings. Rawhide must be cut very thin. One method is to use a sharp knife and a peg driven into a wood block. The distance between the knife blade and the peg is the width desired for the string. Long lengths of rawhide can be cut from a deer hide in this manner, but cut from the belly side rather than the back where the hide is too thick for good string making. Small animal skins also make excellent rawhide for this procedure. Squirrel was often used, and some of the best are raccoon and groundhog. Groundhog is probably the single best rawhide material source. A suitable string can be made from an even smaller section of rawhide by cutting in a spiral, again using the knife and peg. Usually two, or even three, very thin strands of rawhide were utilized to create the string. The width of the strips is determined by the bow's draw weight. You'll have to experiment to determine the correct widths for your bow. The wet, cut strips are fastened to an overhead object, such as a tree limb, or to a nail driven into the side of a building. A heavy weight is tied to the bottom of the strips and the weight turned to tightly twist the strands into a smooth tube. The weight should then be anchored into place until the spirals dry and set. The result is a fairly uniform tube or string. Apply animal grease or beeswax to the string to protect it from the weather.

Rawhide shrinks when it dries, which will shorten the string length. Take this in consideration when cutting the string. You may have to experiment. It's best to make it a bit long, and then cut it again to adjust to the proper length. String also shortens as it is twisted and you can adjust

Loops or knots were usually formed in the damp materials.

the length somewhat by simply twisting the string. The loops or knots must also be formed in the rawhide string before it sets up and dries. Occasionally thin strips of tanned leather were also used as bowstrings and these were also twisted in the same manner.

GUT

Gut strings were also fairly common. Bear, elk, and deer gut were used for the strings. The guts were cleaned inside out, cut into strips, and then twisted to create the string. Gut strings were often single-ply but two-ply strings were also made. Gut is quite easy to use, once you get past the cleaning stage. And, it makes a very durable and smooth string with few lumps. Gut isn't, however, quite as strong as rawhide.

While still wet, or better yet, damp, the gut is cut into strips. Gut strings are made basically in the same manner as rawhide ones. Attach the strands to something solid and pull and twist them to form a tight, evenly shaped tube. Pull and twist until there is no stretch left and then tie off and allow to dry. Again, beeswax or grease is used to lubricate the string and add protection.

In both cases, the loops or knots can be formed in place with the wet materials if you know the string length and can approximate any shrinkage. Alternatively, you can rewet the ends and create the loops after the strings have dried.

SINEW

Sinew was also one of the most common bowstring materials. The sinew was collected from deer or antler legs or backs. Sinew is also an excellent material for creating today's homemade bowstrings. The raw materials are collected, dried or frozen, and then pounded to break down the strands or fibers. The fiber bundles are then pulled apart to produce the thin fiber strands needed to make the string. Because of their longer lengths, back tendons make the best sinew for bowstrings. Once the sinew fibers have

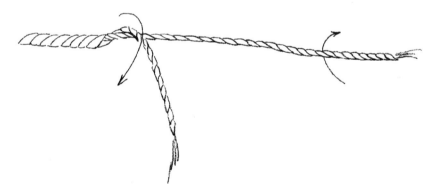

Sinew was also often formed into bowstrings. The sinew is pulled apart into thin fiber strands and woven in a manner called the "reverse twist." Tie two sections together with a knot. Separate these into a top and bottom section. Twist the top section clockwise, then bring the top section down over the bottom section counterclockwise. Twist what is now the top section clockwise and bring it down over the other strand counterclockwise. To add a new section insert it between the top and bottom strands and twist in place.

been separated into strands the thickness of heavy thread, you're ready to begin twisting them into a string.

The most common method of assembling the strands is the reverse twist. Two strands are twisted individually clockwise. Then the two strands are twisted together counterclockwise. This creates a string that wants to hold together. To accomplish this, tie the two sections together with a knot. It's best to have one section shorter than the other for ease in joining other sections. Separate into top and bottom sections. Twist the top section clockwise, and then bring the twisted top string down over the front of the lower string counterclockwise. This puts the lower section on top. Twist it clockwise and then bring it back down over the now-bottom string, twisting these two tightly together. Continue until you reach the end of a section. To add a new section, insert it between the top and bottom sections and twist in place.

PLANT MATERIALS

Plant materials, including those readily available to the Native Americans, can be used to create bowstrings. Tough fibrous

Plant materials were also spun into strands using a drop-spindle, and then using the reverse twist method of twining them together.

plants include hemp, nettles, palm, yucca, cattail, dogbane, milkweed, and flax. The inner bark of several trees can also be turned into serviceable cordage. These include elm, willow, cedar, juniper, mesquite, wild cherry, and cottonwood.

To create cordage, the plant materials can be broken into fibers and twisted in the same manner as for making bowstrings. These are not, however, quite as strong as the animal fibers. The trick in creating a strong bowstring is to make several small twisted strands, then twist them together to create the final string. A better tactic is to use a spinning device to create the strands. An antique spinning wheel does a great job of creating endless strands for making up these types of strings. A simple drop-spindle, as used by many "primitive" people, can also be used to create cordage for a bowstring.

A variety of loops and knots were used to fasten the string to the bow.

FINISHING

A bowstring made of either sinew or plant fibers ends up with tiny burrs sticking out everywhere. Major protrusions can be cut off with a sharp knife. Applying animal grease or beeswax will help lay down the tiny burrs and smooth up the string. This also adds protection to the string.

LOOPS AND KNOTS

A variety of knots as well as loops were used to hold the string on the bow, depending on whether the bow tips were nocked or not. Loops tend to last longer than knots, but are somewhat harder to fit in the initial stage. A common method was to use a permanent knot on the lower limb and a loop on the top to be slid in place when bracing the bow.

ENDLESS STRINGS

Modern day strings are created using an "endless" technique. Some ancient bowstrings were also created in this manner. You can use homemade natural spun plant or animal fibers or manufactured natural fibers to create these types of strings. You can also use modern-day string materials, most commonly Dacron bowstring.

Whatever the material, the string is made by wrapping the string around a form in the number of strands needed, then tying off. The ends are then "served" or wrapped to form loops, and the middle area (on modern strings) served for the arrow nocking position.

The simplest method is to drive spike nails into a 2 by 4 to hold the string-length loops. A bowstring jig makes the chore easier if you intend to make several strings. Whether you use a simple spike method or the jig, the holding nails or pegs should be the exact distance apart you wish the bowstring length to be. Normally this will average about 4 inches less than the bow, but it can be longer or shorter.

Tie the string strand to one post or nail and begin winding around the two until you reach the number of strands required to give the necessary strength for your particular bow weight. If using natural, homemade, or purchased materials, you'll have to use the trial-and-error method. If using purchased Dacron bowstring materials, follow the chart included with the packaging.

Once the string has been wrapped, clip off the end, untie the starting end from the post, and tie the two together. Now rotate the strands around the pegs or nails until the knot is about ¾ inch from one of the pegs.

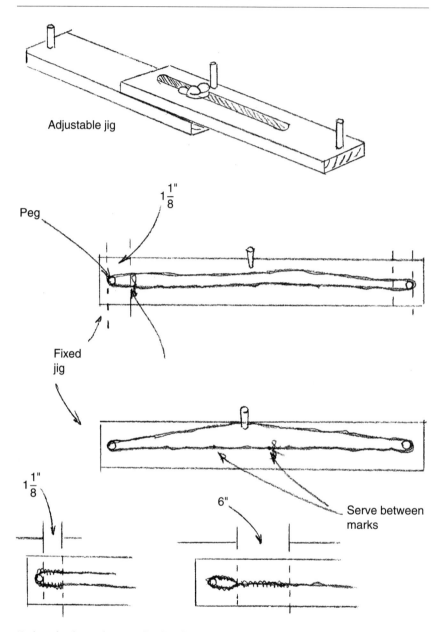

Adjustable jig

Peg

$1\frac{1}{8}$"

Fixed
jig

$1\frac{1}{8}$"

6"

Serve between
marks

Modern day bowstrings are "endless" strings made of Dacron bowstring materials. A simple jig can be used to create the strings, winding the string around the pegs to achieve the number of loops desired.

Using a marking pencil, mark the lengths you wish the loops to be on each end. Make the marks ¼ inch longer than the finished loop should be, and rotate the strings around the pegs until the marked areas of the loops are in the center of the form board. Pull one side over the spreader loop and out of the way. Now you're ready to "serve" or wrap one of the loops. This can be done with ordinary heavy-duty cotton thread, but I prefer rod-winder's thread because it's stronger. It's much easier to make neat wraps if you use a simple bobbin made of a piece of heavy-duty wire and a long bolt through the thread spool.

Wax the string between the marks first with string maker's wax, then start winding serving thread around the strings, keeping the serving neat and tight. Twist twice for extra strength. Tie with a fisherman's blind knot, and then rotate the string around the pegs until you can serve around the other end loop. Rotate string back into position with loops around the end pegs. The ends should be offset about ¼ inch from the loop by tying the strings together in the same manner, serving the loop about 6 inches down on the string. Repeat the process on the opposite

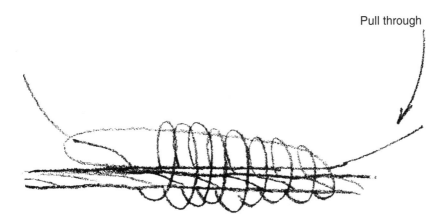

Serve or wrap the end loops using a blind fisherman's knot to tie off. Apply beeswax to finish off the string.

end, then remove the string from the right-hand peg, twist clockwise for a dozen turns, and replace back on the peg. Mark about 4 inches from either side of the center of the string, apply wax, and serve this area. As a final step, apply a tiny bit of glue to the ends of the servings, and wax with beeswax.

Chapter
15

QUIVERS AND SUCH

Although paintings of Native Americans hunting buffalo from horseback sometimes illustrated the scene with arrows held in their teeth, quivers for holding arrows, along with bow cases, were also very necessary Native American weapons accessories. You'll need the same for your own primitive-style bow and arrows.

A variety of quiver styles and materials were used. Actually, the Native Americans used the skin of just about any critter, fur or hair on, or dehaired for quivers. Shown is a sample of a Native American–style quiver made by Randall "Hutch" Hutchison.

Quivers were separate, or sometimes made in conjunction with a case to protect the bow, all being lashed together in one "travel" or storage piece.

A wide variety of materials were used for quivers, including rawhide and tanned skins with the hair on, such as deer, elk, buffalo, beaver, otter, moose, wolf, and others. Tanned leathers were also used in many instances. Deerskin was a favorite tanned leather for quivers. Some quivers were rather primitive; others were extremely well made and decorated with quill or beadwork.

An arrow quiver or quiver and bow case for your own use can also be made from a variety of materials and be as plain or as decorative as you wish. Shown are three basic styles, a rawhide belt quiver, a hair-on back quiver, and a Plains-style quiver-bow case.

RAWHIDE BELT QUIVER

Rawhide was a very popular material with the Native Americans because it is much like today's plastics. It can be formed into any number of items while wet and when it dries, it shrinks and maintains the form that has been created. When it gets wet again, it

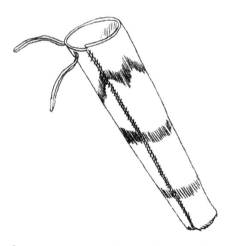

loses its shape once more. But the Native Americans had a solution for that as well.

The pattern shown is a fairly typical design. You can alter it to suit, including the length to fit your particular type of arrows. Make a paper pattern, cut out around the pattern, and then transfer it to the rawhide piece. Use a felt-tip marking pen to make

One very common style quiver was the rawhide belt quiver.

the outline. Then dampen or soak the rawhide to make it pliable. Cut the "tube" and bottom pieces to shape with a sharp craft or utility knife. Use a leather punch to punch holes for lacing the pieces together.

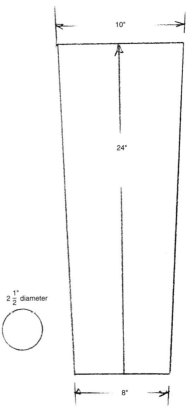

The next step is to cut the lacings. The lacings can also be thin strips of rawhide. One method of cutting a continuous strip for lacing is to use a nail driven into a board with a knife blade also pushed into the board. The distance between the knife blade and the nail is the width desired. You can actually make a spiraling cut starting on the outside edge of a circle of rawhide, cutting to the center in this manner and

Rawhide belt quiver pattern.

creating a long piece of lacing. Use the knife to cut a starting strip, then position and pull the strip through the nail and knife, turning the circle of rawhide as you go. Note: The rawhide will have to be dampened or wet in order to successfully cut it.

Once you have the tube, bottom, and lacings cut, you will need to shape the wet rawhide around a form. A section of sapling, smoothed and without the bark, is a good choice. One excellent material is a section of elm limb. When elm dies, the bark immediately falls off revealing a very smooth wood surface. A section of cottonwood or sycamore limb can also be smoothed very easily with a drawknife and used as the form. It will take a bit

Make a paper pattern for the pieces from the pattern shown. Transfer these to a piece of damp rawhide and using a sharp knife to cut out the pieces.

Punch holes for lacing the pieces together using a leather lacing punch.

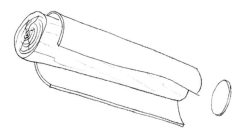

Shape the wet rawhide around a wooden form and lace it together with buckskin laces.

of trial and error to come up with the right size and shape for the form. The form should be slightly smaller than the finished wet rawhide quiver. Use the wet rawhide lacings and an awl to push the lacing through the holes to lace the pieces together. Start with the bottom, lacing it to the end of the tube and then lace up the side. Slide the laced tube over the sapling and allow it to dry overnight. Occasionally move it around the tube to make sure it doesn't dry and shrink too tightly on the sapling to the point you can't get it off. As the quiver begins to dry to a round shape, remove it from the form.

To protect the quiver from dampness, as well as to provide decoration, the quiver can be "sized." Designs can first be painted onto the quiver using acrylic paints. Most natural pigments were somewhat duller than today's modern versions, so you may wish to add a bit of white pigment to the colors to lighten them. A tanned leather tie strap is fastened to the top edge for tying the quiver to a belt. Then size the quiver with two coats of shellac. This will make the rawhide less susceptible to dampness. Cut the tie strap to size and shape from a piece of tanned leather. Punch holes for the location of the strap and fasten it into place with thongs.

HAIR-ON BACK QUIVER

A tanned hair-on back quiver was also extremely common. These quivers were softer than the hard rawhide cases and were more comfortable carried across the back with a strap. Any hair-on pelt can be used for this type of quiver. A coyote skin is just about the correct size and looks "authentic." You can, if you wish,

A tanned, hair-on back quiver is also an interesting project. They are softer than the rawhide quivers. Any hair-on pelt can be used.

keep the coyote face on the bottom of the quiver if desired. Or you can cut off the face and tail, square up the pelt, and use it in that form. Turn the pelt skin side out and mark the outline of the pattern onto the skin. Hold the pelt on a smooth flat board and cut the excess from the pelt using a sharp knife. Punch lacing holes through the pelt. You will also have to punch holes through the pelt at the top and bottom edges for the shoulder strap.

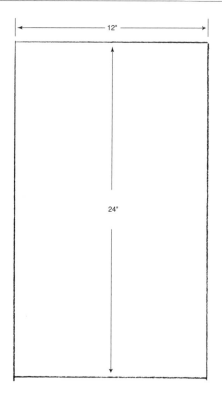

Hair-on back quiver pattern.

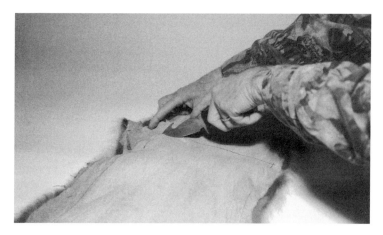

Transfer the pattern to the back, or flesh side of the pelt, and cut it out with a sharp knife.

In this case, the quiver is sewn together wrong side out, then turned right side out after it is finished. The quiver can be laced with buckskin thongs, or sewn with natural or artificial sinew. Some of these types of quivers were laced with buckskin right side out and the lacings were left long as fringe. A fringe piece was sometimes added to the bottom as well. A piece of buckskin, cut from the back of the skin for strength, is used as the shoulder strap. Tie the shoulder strap in place with buckskin lacing.

Punch holes for the lacing.

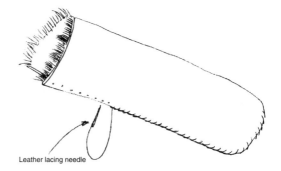

Leather lacing needle

Lace the quiver together wrong side out, then turn the quiver right side out.

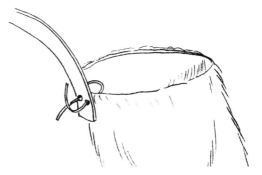

Add the shoulder strap, lacing it in place with buckskin thongs.

BRAIN-TANNED BUCKSKIN QUIVER AND BOW CASE

Quiver and bow case combinations were quite common and ranged from the basic to extremely elaborate using painted designs, beadwork, quillwork, fringe, tassels, and other decorations. Shown is a basic case. You can add almost any decoration you desire.

If you're really a purist, you may wish to do your own brain tanning of skins from deer you've taken. Brain tanning buckskin is not a particularly difficult job, although it does take quite a bit of work, and some time.

TANNING

The first step is to dehair the hide. Traditional buckskin was dehaired in one of two methods. One was to lace the hide to a wooden frame, or peg the hide to the ground and use a scraper to

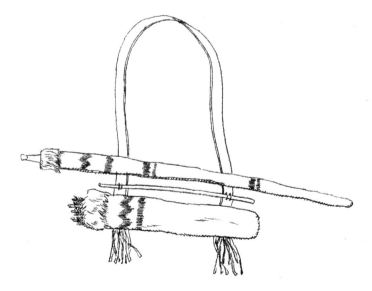

One of the most popular Plains tribe–style quivers also held the bow in a protective case. These cases were made of brain-tanned buckskin.

first remove all fat, meat, and membrane from the flesh side of the hide. Then the hide was turned and the hair removed by scraping as well. You really have to put your back into this type of dehairing. Any holes in the skin must first be sewn together or you will make them larger with the pressure applied on the skin. Another, easier, but equally smelly method was simply to soak the hides in warm water until the hair began to slip. The easiest and quickest method, however, is to first soak the skins in a weak solution of lye water. The lye water can be made from wood ashes. About 3 gallons of fresh, dry wood ashes, without any charcoal chunks are required to do a deer hide. Add about 1½ gallons of ashes to each 5 gallons of water needed to cover the hides in a plastic or wooden tub. Stir thoroughly to dissolve the ashes. Place an egg in the ashes; it should float. If it doesn't float, add more ashes. You can also use ¼ cup of lye dissolved in 10 gallons of

The first step in tanning is to dehair the hide. Soaking in a solution of lye and water loosens the hair. The hair is then removed with a scraper.

The dehaired hide is neutralized in a water bath and liquefied brain matter rubbed into the hide on both sides. Then soak the hide in a solution of brain matter and water.

water. Mix the solution with caution, following instructions on the label. Wear a long-sleeved shirt, rubber gloves, an apron, and eye protection when working with lye.

Place the hide in the solution and weight it down with a rock so it doesn't float. Keep the hide in the solution until the hair slips easily when pulled, usually about a week to ten days, depending on the weather. Wear rubber gloves for the task. Stir the solution several times each day to keep the hide working evenly.

Then, use a scraper to remove all hair. It's extremely important to remove all the epidermis or upper grain layer from the hide. All flesh, fat, and membrane on the flesh side of the hide must be removed as well.

If the hide is dehaired by dry scraping only, warm water is used to plump up the hide for tanning. If lye or ashes are used to loosen the hair, a neutralizing bath is required. The neutralizing

Wring the hide out and string it on a stretching frame. Then use a softening tool to completely stretch and break the hide fibers, until the hide is soft and dry.

bath consists of 10 gallons of water to which 3 gallons of vinegar have been added. Allow the hide to soak overnight, then remove the hide, dump the neutralizing solution, and wash the hide in several changes of water. Wring dry, removing as much water as possible.

The next step is "braining." Native Americans used a mixture of materials, including the brains and ground-up liver from the animal killed. Caution: These days with the possibility of chronic wasting disease (CWD), most experts and biologists suggest avoiding contact with the brains or spinal fluids of deer or elk. I've substituted calf and pork brains and liver, although the liver doesn't work as well as the brain matter.

The brains should be placed in a cloth bag and boiled for about an hour. Do this outside over a camp stove or fish fryer and use an old pot. Remove the bag, retaining the hot liquid. Allow the brains to cool long enough to handle the bag, then open the bag and force the brain matter into a glass or plastic container. Pour half of the brain matter back into the cooked liquid. Half of the brain matter is then worked into the hide by hand. Use rubber or latex gloves. The other half of the brain matter, mixed in the cooked liquid, is later used to cover the hide.

You can also simply place the brains in extremely hot tap water and smash them with your hands. You will need enough liquid to cover the hide for the final step and this will require about 2 gallons of liquid. Regardless of the method used, the brain matter must be applied warm.

Next, rub the brain matter thoroughly into the hide on both sides. Place the hide in a tub and cover with the remaining brain solution. Allow this to sit for several hours or, better yet, overnight. The hide will absorb most of the brain materials.

Remove the hide from the brain solution and thoroughly wring it to remove as much moisture as possible. Restring the hide on the stretching frame, and then use a softening tool to thoroughly work the brain material further into the hide and to stretch and break the fibers. Continue to do this every 15 to 20 minutes or so, take a rest and repeat until the hide is soft and dry. This step is best done with the frame in the shade so the hide doesn't dry too quickly.

Another method is to wring as much moisture as possible from the hide, and then pull it back and forth over a hemp rope strung tautly between trees. A wire cable can also be used for this chore. You can also work the hide back and forth over a breaking stake such as used for modern-day tanning.

The tanned hides will have a bright, white appearance and, if allowed to get wet, will dry hard again. The Native Americans took another step; smoke was also used to cure the hides. This not only made the skins more water-resistant, but also added color

The tanned hide is then smoked over a low, smoky fire to make it more water resistant, and to provide the buckskin color.

and "aroma." I have also smoke-cured deerskins tanned by the modern methods to change them from the white stage to buckskin color and also to add more moisture resistance.

A tripod of thin wooden saplings can be used to smoke the hides. The idea is to create a small and slow fire, feeding it with green, rotten, and/or damp wood to maintain a slow but steady smoke. Do not use soft woods that contain pitch or resin for the fire; the fire should also not be hot enough to cook the skins. One method of making sure the fire doesn't get too hot is to dig a trench under and out from the tripod, build a fire in the trench, and cover the trench with boards. Leave the area under the tripod open and the smoke will come up through the opening. The skins are fastened on the tripod with nails or string. First one side is smoked, then the hides are turned over and the other side smoked.

A wooden box can be built or even a large cardboard box can be used for smoking, as in smoking meat. Place the box over the opening at the end of the trench, lay the hides across sticks in the top of the box, and smoke the hides. The amount of smoking time will vary from a day to three or more. When smoked properly, the hides will turn a nice tan color.

Once the smoking is complete, rinse the hides and then stake or stretch them again to resoften. Finish the flesh side of the hides by rubbing with thin sandpaper. The Native Americans thinned the thicker portions of the hides by working them with sharp shells and flint bone scrapers.

MAKING THE QUIVER AND BOW COVER

You should adjust the pattern shown to suit your arrow length, the number of arrows to be carried, and your bow size. Then lay the buckskin out on a smooth flat surface, flesh side up, and lay the pattern on top of the buckskin. Mark around the pattern with a

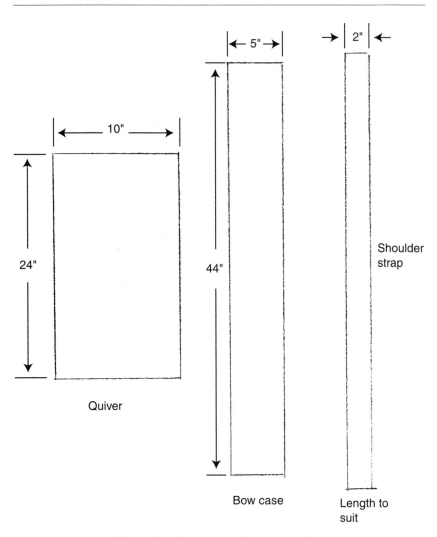

Plains tribe–style quiver and bow case pattern.

sharp felt-tip pen. Cut the buckskin to the correct shape and size following the pattern.

Sew the quiver together wrong side out using sinew. Or you can lace up the quiver right side out with buckskin thongs. The latter were often left long as fringe pieces.

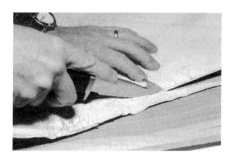

Adjust the pattern to suit your bow and arrow lengths and place it on the flesh or back side of the tanned buckskin and mark around the pattern. Then cut out with a sharp knife.

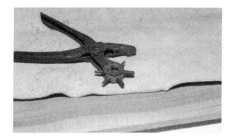

Punch holes with a leather punch, and then sew the quiver together wrong side out with sinew, artificial sinew, or lace with buckskin thongs. Assemble the bow case in the same manner.

Sew or lace the bow case in the same manner. The quiver and bow case are then tied together so the bow and arrows can all be carried or stored together. These Plains-style cases often had a stick tied or sewn between the two to act as a separator and to hold the quiver rigid when all the arrows were removed. A shoulder strap is then sewn in place. In many instances, these straps were fairly wide. Sashes, tassels, paint, or beads were added as decoration.

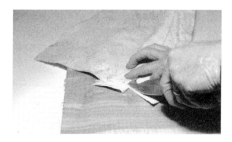

Then assemble the two together and add a shoulder strap. Add tassels, beadwork, painted designs, or fringe as desired. If you desire fringe, you may wish to leave the edge longer and cut the fringe pieces before assembling.

Part V

Food Gathering, Cooking, and Other Tools

The Native Americans were very adept at "scrounging." They used the materials that were on hand for hunting as well as for gathering food. For the most part, the tribes subsisted on hunting, fishing, and food gathering. Some of the eastern tribes, as well as some of the southwestern tribes, later developed agricultural practices. They raised crops for food and stored them for future use. Food-gathering and agricultural artifacts, although not as "glamorous" as arrow and spear points, were just as essential to survival. To truly understand the primitive peoples, you should also try your hand at some of the ancient skills used in making food-gathering and cooking tools.

Chapter
16

BASKETS

Baskets were some of the earliest "tools." Artifacts give us evidence that baskets were in use before pottery was developed. They were used for a variety of purposes, including to carry or hold harvested or gathered food items. Baskets were relatively lightweight, easy to transport, and could hold quantities of

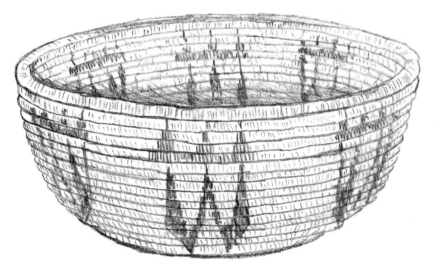

Food gathering tools were essential to survival for Native Americans. These ranged from baskets to pots to digging tools.

berries, fruits, nuts, or roots. Some baskets had slings that could be looped over the shoulders, freeing the hands for gathering. In many instances the foods gathered had to be transported some distance from the village or camp. Tumplines, which are straps or slings passed around the chest or forehead allowing the burden basket to be more easily carried, were also commonplace on many baskets. The shape and size varied greatly from huge "people-sized" baskets to tiny flat "trays" used for serving foods.

Native American basketry became, and still is, a fine example of "utilitarian" art. Beautiful designs were woven into many baskets, the designs often an indicator of the region, tribe, or individual maker. Not only were geometric designs utilized, but also beautiful pictorials were popular.

Baskets were made of many materials. Grasses, reeds, and canes were very common, as were roots, vines, and the shoots from willow, redbud, and witch hazel. The inner bark of cedars, wild cherry, and spruce were often used. My uncle Mike taught me how to obtain and use these materials many years ago. Fibers obtained from the yucca and hemp plants were also utilized. The eastern tribes pounded and separated the wood from oak, hickory, and ash to create thin strips that could be plaited to create baskets.

Three basic techniques were used in creating baskets: coiling, twining, and plaiting.

COILING

One of the most popular methods of basket construction was coiling. These baskets were made of grasses, leaves, wood strips, roots, and fibers. The coiled basket is made in much the same manner as a coiled clay pot. These baskets were extremely tightly woven, some lined and coated with pitch, and were used to hold water. Coiling can be done in several ways. The traditional meth-

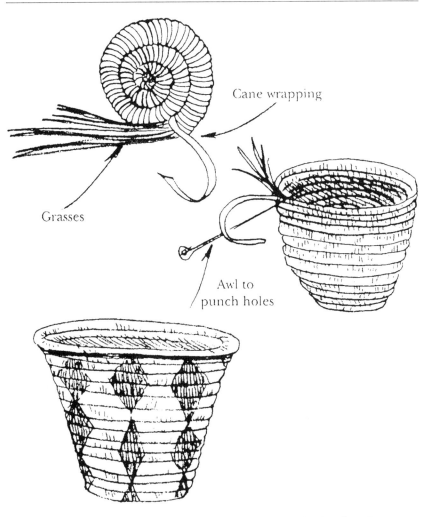

Baskets were made in several different ways. Coiling, or twisting bundles of grasses or fibers together and stitching these with reeds or other materials, was a very popular method.

ods included fiber bundle coiling, five-rod coiling, three-rod coiling, and one-rod coiling.

Fiber bundle construction is simple, but elegant. A bundle or handful of grasses or leaves is wrapped with a lashing of tree roots, cane, or reeds. This wrapped bundle is then formed into a coil with the bottom a solid spiral coil. After the spiral is started, the lashing is wrapped around the outside of the bundle, then laced through the next inside coil and pulled tightly to hold the coils together. A small bone or wooden awl was used to thread

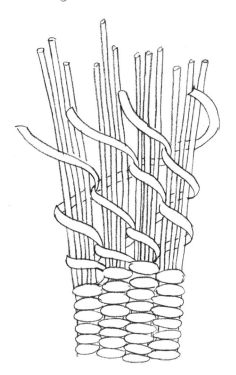

the cane through and tie the pieces together. A leather awl can also be used for the purpose. As more grasses are added to the coil, it is wrapped with the cane, lashing the coils together as the material is wrapped. Once the bottom is completed, the coils are then started up to make the sides and the sides are constructed in the same basic manner. In some instances, a rod was added inside the fiber bundle to add rigidity.

Horizontal rods were also often woven together with vertical wrappings of yucca leaves or other materials to create baskets. Typical patterns were three-rod and five-rod coiling.

In the case of rod coil weaving, willow or other shoots were used as the horizontals with cane, sumac, yucca leaves, or other materials used to "wrap" the coils and hold them together. The rod numbers in the coil were usually one, three, or five.

TWINED BASKETS

These are soft, flexible baskets often made for utility pack baskets, and other transportation purposes. Twined baskets are woven utilizing vertical warps with twine wefts woven around each other as

Soft, flexible baskets were also woven together of a variety of twine materials. Several different twine patterns were used.

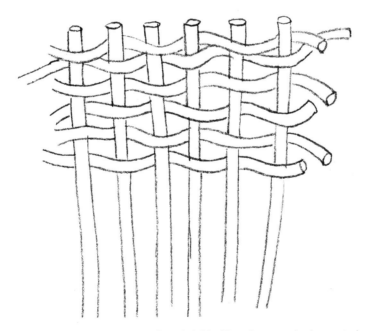

Wicker-style baskets, woven of semi-rigid willow shoots and other materials were also common.

they are woven around and between the warps. Several different patterns were used. On the plain twine method, the wefts are twisted between each warp. In the twill twine method, each twist of the weft pieces wraps two or more warps. This creates a pattern that resembles courses of overlapping bricks. Open twine has the separated warps held in place with separated twined wefts. Wrap twine utilized stiffer warps held together with flexible wefts. These were often root or willow baskets.

More open mesh-style baskets were made using cane, roots, vines, and/or willow shoots. These were used to hold less fine objects, such as nuts, clams, or fruits. These baskets can be made entirely out of cane or semi-rigid pieces of thin wood strips such as willow shoots. The baskets were made by weaving pliable strips, such as cane or roots around the semi-rigid willow shoots. In some instances, the bottoms of these baskets were made of wood. The willow shoots were inserted in holes in the wooden bottom. These baskets were then called "wicker" in some instances.

PLAITED BASKETS

Cane or the pliable inner bark of trees, such as cedar or wild cherry, as well as splits of hickory, were often woven or rather "plaited" into baskets. The bark strips are first pounded or soft-

Plaited baskets were woven of the inner bark of trees such as wild cherry or cedar.

ened, and then simply woven so the warp and wefts cross each other, alternating passing over and under each other. The result is a checkerboard effect. If the basket is to be square or rectangular shaped, a mat is first woven the size of the bottom. Then the warp materials are bent upward and the plaiting continued up the sides. Cylindrical baskets begin with the bottom warps arranged like the spokes of a wheel. After the bottom diameter is reached, the warps are again bent up and the plaiting continued up the sides. Designs were often created by introducing different colored strands. If the basket flares outward, additional warps are added to create the outward shape.

Plaiting consists of two distinct types: plain plaiting and twill plaiting. Plain plaiting results in the simple checkerboard pattern. Mat, square, and rectangular baskets were often made in this manner. Twill plaiting utilizes varying numbers and sequences of the warps and wefts. For instance, a herringbone has two splints crossing each time. Diagonal weaves are possible with this method as well.

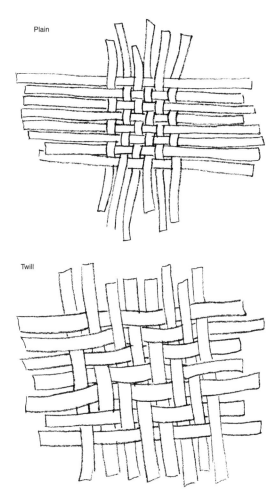

Plaiting is done in two distinct styles: (a) plain and (b) twill.

Chapter

17

POTTERY

Pottery was, and still continues to be, a fine example of beautiful Native American art. Pottery was used to create bowls,
containers, and items for cooking, food storage, and preparation
as well as for eating. Pottery was also used to create effigies, pipes,
and personal adornment objects. We had a natural clay bank near
our home, and making items from clay dug from the bank was
one of my favorite pastimes as a youngster.

Two basic methods are used in creating pottery in the Native
American manner: coiling or modeling. These methods were
often combined along with "paddling" the material into a shape.

COILING

Coiling is an ancient art the Pueblos still use to make elegant pottery. A piece of clay is flattened, and then the edges shaped into a
round to create the bottom. This bottom piece is then placed inside a shallow basket or flat bowl so that as it is worked on the pottery can be turned. A ball of clay is then rolled out into a thick
ropelike coil. This coil is gently pressed into place around the
upper edge of the clay bottom. Another roll or coil is created and
layered on top of the first. Joints are staggered so no two joints of

Pottery was and still is one of the best examples of beautiful Native American art. A wide variety of items were made from clay.

The most common method of constructing pots was coiling.

Ropes of clay are coiled to create the shape of the pot or object.

the coils meet in the same spot. As each layer or coil is added, it's pressed down, and then pinched in to meet the one below it. This adheres the coils together. As the coils are added upwards, they are also squeezed between the thumb and fingers to thin the sides of the pot to the desired thickness. Fingers are dipped into water before smoothing the cracks between the coils. The pot is turned around on the basket or shallow bowl to allow for working evenly on all sides. As the pot walls rise, they are shaped inward or outward as desired. The sides are smoothed using rounded pieces of shell, gourd, or broken pottery pieces. One hand is held inside the pottery to hold the walls while the smoothing object is worked on the outside. Small coil pottery pieces are often completed in one sitting. Larger pieces will slump with the weight of the coils. They must frequently be allowed to dry slightly before the upper coil layers are added.

The cracks between the coils are smoothed inside and out.

MODELING

Modeling was a method used by many eastern tribes. In modeling, a large piece of thinned clay is placed over a mold, usually an inverted jar or bowl. The mold with the clay on it is turned and modeled or shaped by patting with the hands, a smooth flat stone, or a paddle. Once the clay begins to harden enough to support itself, it is removed from the mold and placed on a woven fiber ring or shallow bowl. A smooth anvil stone is held against the inside while a wooden paddle is used on the outside to thin and further refine the shape of the pottery.

Many times a combination of the two methods was used; for instance, modeling the lower portion of the pottery where it flares outward. When the pottery begins to neck down, coils are used to create this portion. The coils are placed and modeled in the same manner as for basic coil work,

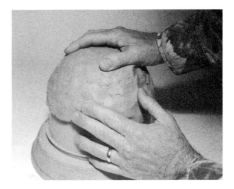

Modeling was another tactic, shaping the clay over a form, such as an inverted bowl.

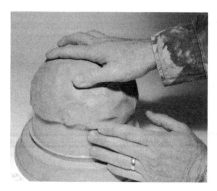

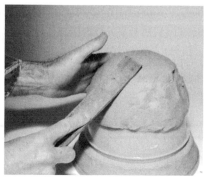

Once the clay is in place, smooth it down into a rough shape.

As the clay begins to harden, the object is placed on a flat surface such as a fiber or wood ring. It is then "paddled" with a wooden paddle to smooth it up.

Continue turning the pot around and smoothing it with the paddle.

Use a sharp knife to cut the "top" smooth and even.

except anvil stones and paddles are often used to smooth the joints and finish off the pottery.

DRYING

The pot should be placed in a warm shady spot with plenty of ventilation so it can air-dry, but not dry out so quickly it creates cracks. Air-dry for a day or two or until the pot hardens enough so that it can be handled. The surface is smoothed again, this time using a scraper of a flint chip or bone or a dull knife held at 90 degrees to the surface. Hold your hand inside the pot to provide support while scraping the outside. There will probably be some minor cracks, which can be filled with wet clay. After the pot hardens completely, use sandstone to smooth the surface.

The pot should be allowed to dry in a warm place with plenty of ventilation.

Wipe the surface with a wet cloth to remove the sanding debris. Utility pots were often fired without added decoration.

SLIPPING AND POLISHING

Pots that were to be decorated were given a coat of "slip." This was a creamy mixture of water and clay. Various colored clays were used for creating the slip, including red, white, yellow, or tan to give the pot an even color and smooth surface for painting on decorations. The semi-liquid slip is wiped onto the surface with a soft rag, making sure it fills all pores and indentations. Several coats are applied, allowing the pot to dry between coats. If the pot is not to be painted, before the last coat of slip is completely dry, the pot is polished with a small, very smooth stone. This takes a great deal of time and patience, but results in a shiny, smooth pot.

DECORATING

Pottery decoration consists of painting, impressing, stamping, incising, and engraving. Painting is one of the most common forms of decoration. A feather or the tip of a twig chewed into a fine-shaped brush was often used. Paint was made from a variety of plant sources. The drawings were done freehand. Two other types of painting techniques were also used. Negative painting consists of painting a design in black over the cream- or light-colored slip,

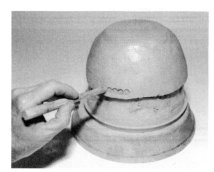
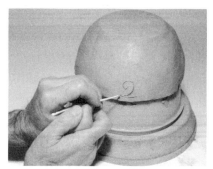

One method of decorating is stamping the soft clay.

Decorations can also be "incised" into the clay.

allowing the lighter color to show through in the desired pattern. A more elaborate form of negative painting is done by first coating a cream or light, slip-colored piece with wax. A design is then cut into the wax, removing the wax where the design will be. The entire piece is then painted black with the paint adhering to the slip. The wax is then removed to reveal the pattern.

Impression and stamping were two other decorating forms and are basically the same technique. A variety of materials is pressed into the still-soft clay to produce a pattern. Examples include shells, paddles with cord wrapped around them, or wooden stamps with designs cut in them. Another type of stamping consisted of rolling a notched wood or shell to create a series of piercings.

Pottery was also incised by using a sharp-pointed wooden or bone tool to cut designs in the soft clay of an unfired pot. After the pot was fired, sharp tools were used to scratch fine lines in the surface, in the manner of engraving.

FIRING

Firing was the most complicated and "delicate" part of pottery making. It is extremely easy to over-fire or under-fire. It is also extremely easy to break or damage a pot. The ancient method is to create a layer of cow or sheep dung about a foot high. Shards or

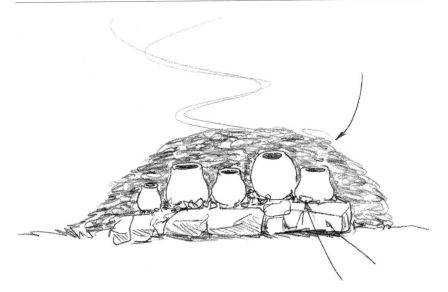

Firing is a very important and delicate part of pottery making. The ancient method utilizes sheep or other dung to provide a smoldering, hot fire.

pieces of broken pottery are placed over the dung. Then the pots are set, upside down, on top of the shards. Shards are also placed over the pots, and more dung piled over the top of the shards. The shards protect the pots from stains caused by the burning dung. The dung burns fairly slowly, but builds up a moderately high heat. Some tribes covered the top with fine damp manure once the fire was started to create a "closed" fire. The damp manure produces a dark, dense smoke, giving the pots a shiny black appearance. If the fire is left open, more air reaches the pots and the resulting color is normally a reddish hue.

Firing can take from an hour to several hours, depending on the number and size of pots, temperature, and humidity. In most instances, the fire was allowed to burn down to nothing but ashes and then the pots cooled before moving them. When the pots are removed from the ashes they are immediately wiped with a bit of animal grease and a cloth or piece of buckskin.

Chapter
18

WOODENWARE

Woodenware was very common and included bowls, spoons, digging tools, and gathering baskets from bark. Digging sticks were also quite common, merely sharpened on one end. Some had crutch-type handles added to the top to provide more leverage. Wooden shovels were also fairly numerous. Mortar and

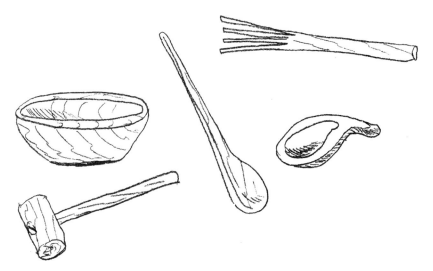

Wood was used for a wide variety of food gathering and cooking tools, and other implements as well. Cooking tools included food hammers, bowls, ladles, and whisks.

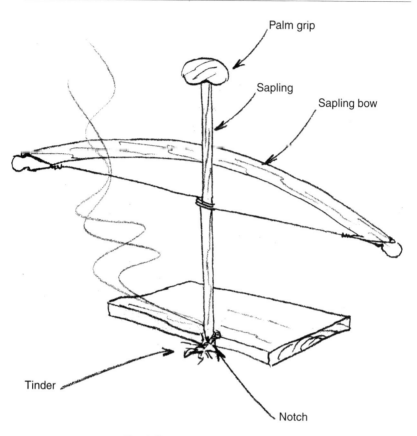

Fire drills were essential to survival.

pestles, although more often made of stone, were also made of wood. A variety of paddles and stirrers were also created for stirring foods in baskets or wooden or pottery bowls. Wooden "whisks" of sapling or roots bent into a rounded shape, similar to modern day utensils, were even in existence. Food hammers, much like today's modern utensils, were also used to pound pemmican. They were also used by the Eskimos to pound blubber to break up the fats. Spoons and ladles were often highly decorated. Wood and bark was also used to create storage vessels.

Probably one of the most important wooden tools was the fire drill, used to start fires. Wood, of course was also used to create housing and shelter and to build furniture. One example is the willow slat bed.

DIGGING AND WOODWORKING TOOLS

Wood handles were used for mattocks, digging tools, axes, and other food gathering and food "manufacturing" tools. In these instances, stone pieces were lashed to the wooden handles with rawhide. One of the most common tools was the adze. These were used in one form or another across most of North America

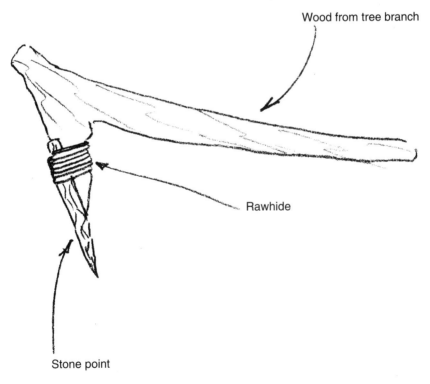

Wood from tree branch

Rawhide

Stone point

Digging tools included mattocks and "hoes."

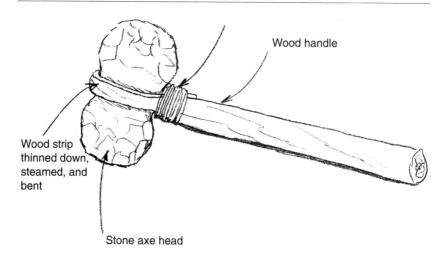

Wood handle

Wood strip
thinned down,
steamed, and
bent

Stone axe head

Axes, as well as adzes, made of stone with wooden handles were important tools for cutting down trees, building dugouts, and other chores.

and were usually a wooden handle to which a stone blade was attached. The blade was often made of shell, bone, or sharpened moose or elk antler.

Axes were also extremely important. These were also commonly made with stone blades, although metal blades became extremely popular in later years. The ancient stone axes utilized a rounded stone with a groove on either side. A sapling was heated and bent around the axe head, and then rawhide was used to tie off the handle.

OTHER TOOLS

Other tools included chisels, gouges, wedges, pump drills, and stone drill points. Arrow and bow-making tools included shaft straighteners, hatchets, and scrapers.

Skin working required scrapers, knives, awls, and needles. The latter were often made from bone or antler sections. (Knives are covered in Section VIII.)

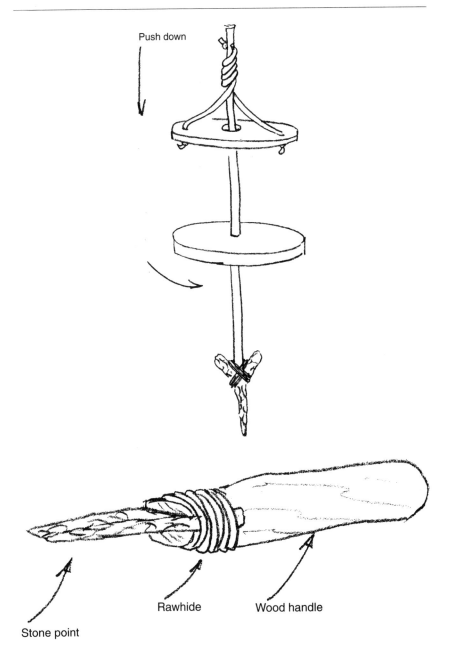

Push down

Stone point

Rawhide

Wood handle

Pump drills (a), chisels (b), gouges, and other tools were used for working wood, bone, shell, and other materials.

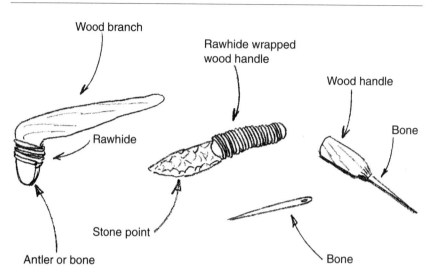

Wood branch

Rawhide wrapped
wood handle

Wood handle

Bone

Rawhide

Stone point

Antler or bone

Bone

Hide-working tools included scrapers, knives, awls, and needles.

Cordage making tools included awls, fiber-spinning spindles, and net bobbins.

Obviously items of great personal satisfaction, many of these tools were finely made. If you're into re-creating the lifestyle, you may wish to make some of these utensils and tools for your own use. They will definitely provide a greater understanding of the ingenuity and craftsmanship of the Native Americans.

Part VI

Fishing Tools

Fish and other water-related species were extremely important foods for the Native Americans. Many of the earlier methods used to catch fish would not be considered "sporting" today, but catching the fish was essential to survival. For instance, certain plants were utilized to stun fish so they would float to the surface, ready to be harvested. A narcotic juice or pulp was extracted from plants, including the stalk and leaves of mullein (often called fish weed) or soap plant. Walnut husks and buckeye seeds were also crushed and used for the purpose.

Other tools are as useful these days as during the earlier times, and some are just fun to make. Make sure you understand state and local game laws regarding the use of some of these tools if you use them for "fishing."

Chapter

19

SPEARS AND HARPOONS

Fish spears, or rather "gigs," were quite common and were used not only for spearing fish, but also for spearing frogs as well. Spears can be whittled from a hardwood stick or sapling, or the tips can be made of bone or antler.

WOOD GIG

The simplest spear is whittled from a sapling. The sapling should provide a straight section 7 to 8 feet long and about 1¼ to 1½ inches in diameter. A piece of hickory is a good choice; ash is another. Use a sharp knife or drawknife to remove the bark and smooth up the sapling to provide a smooth handle. Then split up the smallest end of the sapling to about 7 to 8 inches. Use a piece of hardwood, shaped like a wedge, to force the split pieces apart. This will be a temporary wedge and should be large enough to force the points far enough apart that you can work these points into barbs. Use a sharp knife to shape the split pieces into sharp ends. Cut the backward-facing barbs on the inside edges of both spear points. Finally, shape a permanent hardwood wedge to fit in place between the prongs and below the last barbs cut in the prongs. Glue the wedge in place with pitch. You can also provide

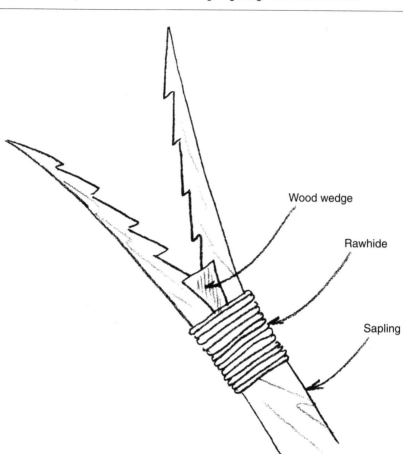

Fish spears or gigs were very common. The simplest is whittled from a sapling, points and all. The points are sharpened, barbs cut in them, and a wooden wedge used to hold them apart.

additional strength by wrapping just below the wedge with strips of the inner bark of wild cherry or basswood. Rawhide wraps can also be used.

DEER LEG BONE GIG

Another simple spear was made from a leg bone of a deer. The spear has a single point. The first step is to cut off the bone ends, leaving the long, straight center portion. In the early days these

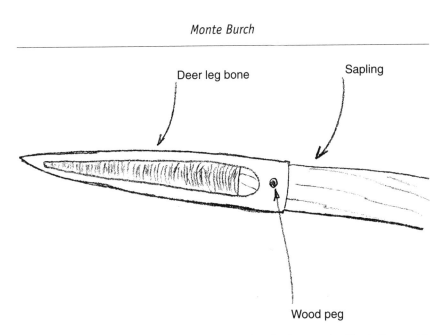

Deer leg bone

Sapling

Wood peg

A deer leg-bone gig has a single point and is quite simple to make. The hollow end is hafted over the reduced end of a wooden handle.

bones were boiled, the meat eaten off them, the ends broken off with rocks, and the marrow sucked out. These days, the marrow can be removed by boiling the bones and using a piece of heavy wire, such as a coat hanger, to push out the marrow. Or do as I do, and simply let your dog chew on the bone.

In any case, the marrow is removed to leave a hollow bone. One end of the bone is sharpened to a point. Traditionally, a large piece of sandstone was used to grind the point sharp. These days, a disc sander makes short work of the chore—but make sure you wear a dust mask and eye protection. Also these days, due to CWD, experts advise against handling the bone marrow. Wear protective disposable latex gloves.

After the point has been shaped, a wooden handle is cut and shaped in the same manner as for the previous spear. The smaller end of the handle is shaped to fit into the back, hollow portion of the point. A hole is bored through the back end of the bone and

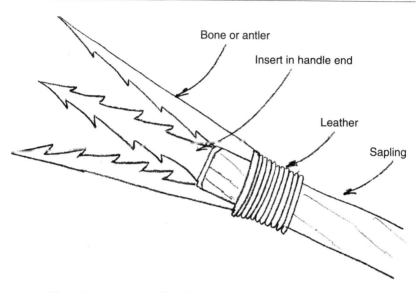

Other gigs and spears utilized bones in either a single or double style.

the wooden handle and a hardwood peg driven in place to secure the bone point to the spear.

BONE POINTS

Shoulder and other solid bones were also shaped into single or double spear or gig points. Single points were made in much the same shape as stone points. They were also hafted to the handle in the same manner. Double-bone and even triple-bone points with barbs ground into them were also fastened to handles with pitch and rawhide.

DEER SHOULDER BLADE GIG

Another type of gig was made from the scapula or shoulder bone of a deer. The outside, thickened edges along with the center, raised ridge were left intact and the thinner portions cut away to produce a three-pronged gig. This was then fastened to a handle or haft with rawhide.

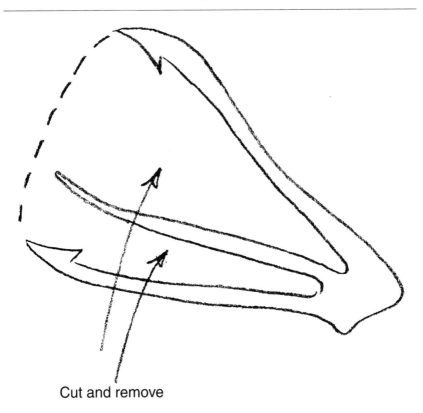

Cut and remove

A deer shoulder bone or scapula makes an excellent fish or frog gig. Cut away the thin inner portions leaving the raised or thicker outer areas.

HARPOONS

Harpoons are spears with removable points. The Native American harpoon points were made of bone, antler, and sometimes stone. Although harpoons are most closely associated with the Eskimos, the coastal tribes, as well as some of the interior tribes, also used them. Harpoons were used not only for gathering fish, such as salmon, but also for hunting water-inhabiting game such as seals, walrus, sea lions, beavers, muskrat, and others.

Many harpoon handles had a hole in the front. The point was loosely inserted into the hole. A cord was lashed to the harpoon and tied to the wooden handle. When the barb stuck a fish or animal, it came loose and the handle rose to the top to provide a "float" to help wear down the animal or fish and also to provide a visible means of location. In other cases, the harpoon was attached to a separate float. Sealskin floats were commonly used with harpoons thrown from kayaks for whales and other large quarry.

Again, the first step is to acquire a straight and sturdy handle. Ash and hickory are good choices because they grow a straight trunk free of lower limbs. Start with an 8-foot piece and you can then adjust to the needed length. Debark and make as smooth as possible. In many instances, a bone "cap" was fastened over the

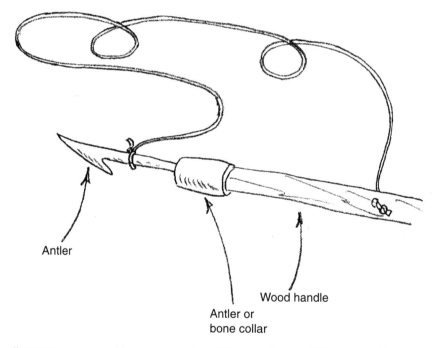

Antler

Wood handle

Antler or
bone collar

Harpoons are spears with removable points. Eskimos and many of the coastal tribes commonly used them. A simple harpoon consists of a handle with a hole in front along with an antler shaped and sharpened to create a spear with a barb. The point is tied to the handle, which acts as a float. Sealskin bladder floats were often attached to harpoon points.

point end. This prevented the point from splitting out the handle when it struck the quarry. The end of the handle is reduced to fit the bone cap, which is made from a femur bone. The bone cap is held in place with pitch and a wooden peg through a hole in the cap and the handle holds the cap in place.

HARPOON POINTS

A number of different style points were used on harpoons. One of the simplest points is made from a small section of antler. The antler section should have a main beam and a point. The area behind the small tine is shaped to a sharp point, and the small tine sharpened as the "barb." The point of the main tine is shaped to fit into the hole in the end of the handle. A groove is cut around the point and a cord tied to it. The cord is then tied to the harpoon handle. The point is loosely fitted into the hole in the end

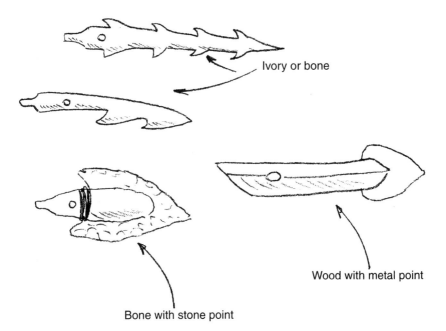

Ivory or bone

Bone with stone point

Wood with metal point

A number of different point designs can be created from antler and bone.

of the handle. Note: The point should slip in and out of the hole in the end of the handle fairly easily. The Eskimos often shaped antler sections into multi-barb harpoon points.

Another type of point utilized a hollow bone with a sharp point on the end. The hollowed section of the bone fit over a smaller section of wood on the handle. The point end of the bone was shaped into a sharp point or had a section of antler, or even a stone point, hafted to it. In some instances, antler sections were sharpened, then the rear of the point hollowed out to fit over the small end of the harpoon handle. The Eskimos and the West Coast tribes often used stone points set in grooves in the front of the main antler point.

Chapter
20

TRAPS AND NETS

Native Americans commonly used traps. The simplest traps were "mazes" or funnels of stones piled to force fish into a small section of water, where they could be speared, hand-grabbed, or netted. Sections of saplings were also driven into the water to create these mazes. I grew up along a river that flooded each spring into small creeks, which also flooded into road ditches and fields. Some folks used sections of metal fencing to block off these small waterways after the flood. When the water receded, the fish that had swum up into these areas were left "high-and-dry." It was illegal, but a traditional method of acquiring fish by many Ozarkers. Some Ozarkers also had wooden fish traps set in many of the rivers. Traps were and are now pretty much illegal for sport fish, but are still used by some commercial fishermen.

The Native Americans made traps of saplings, vines, and reeds lashed into several shapes. The traps were used for anything available in the locale, including fish and lobster.

One of the most ingenious traps is the fish wheel created by the Native Americans of Alaska and Canada. Designed for the rivers of the North, the fish wheel was fashioned on a log raft. A

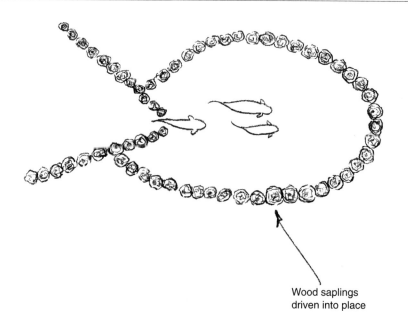

Wood saplings
driven into place

The Native Americans very commonly used traps for fishing. The most common traps were "weirs" used to funnel fish into a shallow area where they could be caught with hands, dip nets, or speared.

series of two to three baskets made of saplings and willow shoots were constructed with an opening in one end. These baskets were fastened to a log axle. The fish wheel/raft was secured in place over a riffle or against a bend in the river where current would turn the wheel. Fish were trapped in the turning basket and, as the basket was lifted out of the water, the fish were dumped through the hole in the end of the basket into a holding box. Naturally, these are also illegal these days.

NETS

Cordage made from native plant materials and woven into a variety of nets, was one of the most common methods of catching fish. A wide variety of nets were used all across the country. These

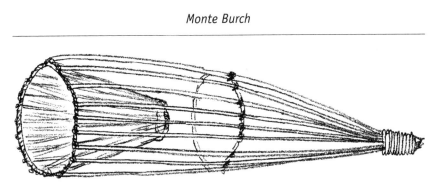

Traps woven of willow shoots and other flexible wood shoots were also common.

included dip nets, cast nets, gill nets, and seines. In fact, the practice of dip netting with large dip nets on some of the major rivers established some of the first "individual property rights" among the Native Americans. Individuals could actually "own" certain sections of the river to dip from. Net making is still an important and fun skill, although most materials will be "modern."

Some nets were woven using bone, antler, or wood shuttles; other nets were simply tied. Although you may wish to experi-

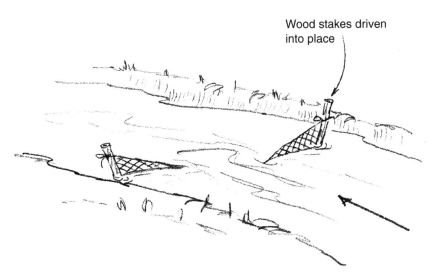

Wood stakes driven
into place

Cordage was made into any number of nets. A gill net was quite common.

ment with spinning natural fibers into strands for weaving, modern-day materials make the chore much easier. Slip Proof Bonded Filament nylon, available from Jann's Netcraft, is a good choice. Following are representative projects.

GILL NET

A gill net (where legal) is an extremely effective tool for gathering fish. It's also fairly easy to assemble. In fact, the basics for tying a gill net can also be used for many other types of nets. The cording is sold in different sizes; a common size is No. 18. The cord that will be the top cord of the net (the suspension line) should be size No. 48. This is tied between two trees or other objects, at about eye level. Core liners, or the "vertical" droppers, are tied using a "girth" hitch with two lines dropping from each knot. An even number of these should be equally spaced along the suspen-

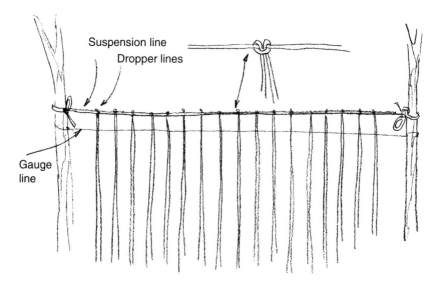

Making a gill net begins with the suspension line or the top of the net tied between two objects at eye level. Vertical droppers or core liners are then tied in place, spaced as desired. A guideline or gauge line tied in place helps gauge the size of the mesh and shows you where to tie the knots.

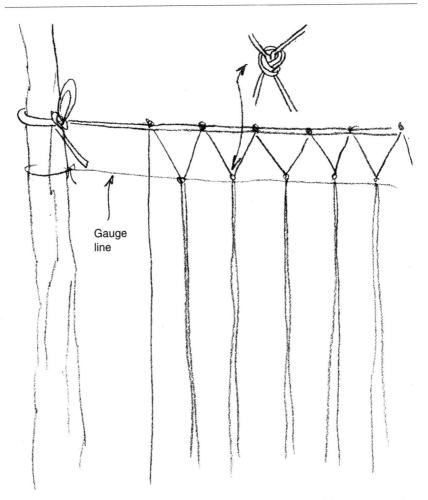

Gauge
line

The first step is to tie the second line to the third using an overhand knot, then continue tying until you reach the next-to-the-last line.

sion line and allowed to hang down. A spacing of 1 inch creates a 1-inch mesh net, although the diamond opening will be 2 inches when stretched out. Their lengths should be plenty long to allow for the knots and spacing and to create the depth of the net needed. To keep the suspension line straight and even, lash a sapling in place and tie the suspension line to it.

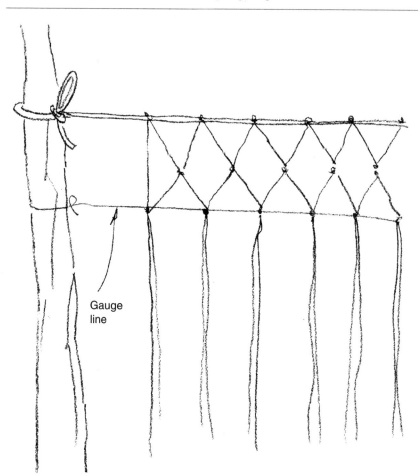

Gauge
line

Lower the guideline and begin tying the next row to the first line. Continue alternating in this fashion to complete the net.

Starting at one end, skip the first line. Grasp the second line and tie it to the third line using an overhand knot. The location of the knot determines the horizontal spacing and this can vary depending on the fish species targeted. It's important to maintain an even spacing, and one method is to tie a spacing guide line in place for the row of knots, then retie this guide line as you move downward. The guide line should be tied on the back of the net so it will be out of your way. Then tie the fourth and fifth, six and seventh lines, and so forth, until you reach the end. The last line on the end will remain untied.

Begin the second row by tying the first and second and so forth. Then again on the third row, skip the first line and tie beginning with the second line. Continue tying until all rows are completed. At the bottom, add another heavier suspension line. You may also wish to add heavier suspension lines on the ends or sides to strengthen them as well.

NET WEAVING WITH A SHUTTLE

You'll need a shuttle and a gauge stick. The shuttle can be whittled from a piece of wood and the gauge stick is simply a 1-inch dowel or sapling. The first step is to learn to make a chain of starting meshes. Wind the twine on the shuttle. Wrap the twine twice

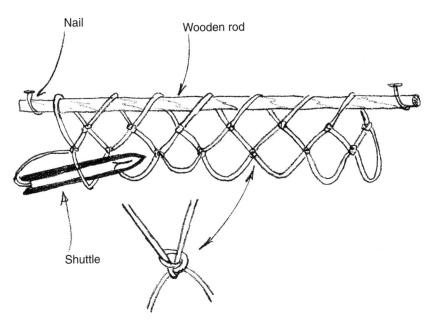

A net can also be woven with a shuttle and a gauge stick.

around the gauge stick and tie it tight. Then tie again. Slip this loop off the gauge stick and hang the upper end on a nail or peg. Pull the gauge stick downward and, at the same time, tie the first mesh knot. Hold the knot in place on the gauge while threading the shuttle through to tie the knot. Continue making a chain of starting meshes. Remove the gauge stick and move it downward, while leaving the starting mesh attached to the nail. As you tie the chain, straighten out the meshes by pulling them outward in both directions.

Once you have the starting chain completed, thread the chain of meshes onto a stiff rod and suspend it from nails or hooks. Begin the second row by wrapping the twine around the gauge stick and pinching it in place as you tie the knots. Leave the new knots in place on the gauge stick until they become over-crowded, and then pull some of them off.

Chapter
21

HOOK AND LINE

Although hook and line is the most common method of fishing these days, it wasn't as "effective" as many of the other methods and was not quite as common to the Native Americans. Artifacts, however, do reveal pre-Columbian fishhooks that were

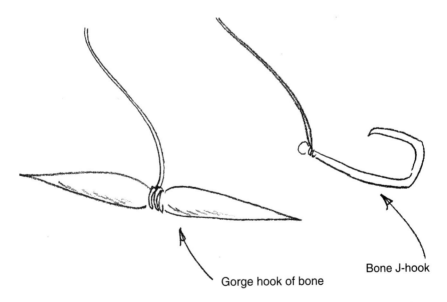

Gorge hook of bone

Bone J-hook

Although hook and line were not as commonly used as other means of fishing, bone hooks were used, the "J" and the "gorge" hooks.

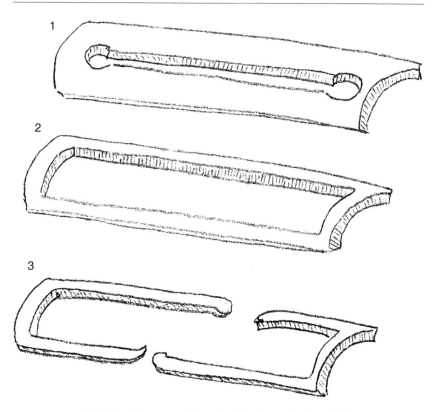

J-style hooks were cut from the wing bone of a large bird.

extremely efficient. The hooks were commonly made of deer or other animal bone, or sometimes of antler. Two types of hooks were used, the family "circle" or "J"-style and "gorge" hooks. The J-style hooks sometimes had barbs cut into them. These were often cut from the toe bone of a deer and were used with bait. The eastern tribes also made hooks from the wing bones of larger birds such as wild turkey and geese. A section was cut from the bone using a stone saw; then, a pump drill was used to bore holes toward the ends. The saw was then used to cut between the holes and a sandstone used to open the hole further. By cutting and shaping an open rectangle was left. This was then cut to create two J-style hooks.

The gorge style hook was the simplest. It normally consisted of an antler, a bone, or even a piece of wood sharpened on both ends. A hole was drilled in the center and a thong tied to it. The hook was buried in some type of bait and the thong tied to a solid object. When the fish swallowed the bait, the hook turned and embedded itself in the throat or stomach of the fish. The critter was then captive. These gorge-style hooks were used to catch birds and animals as well. Sounds cruel, but it was matter of survival.

Part VII

Hunting Tools

The Native Americans utilized many different forms of hunting. Game meat was the primary food for many pre-Columbian tribes and the Eskimos of North America. And the game also provided many other useful products, including leather, fur, bone, and antler. Although any method available at the time was used, Native Americans respected the game and did not wantonly harvest it, as did the invading Europeans. Bows and arrows, spears, harpoons, clubs, bolas and slings, traps, deadfalls, lassos, pits, and snares were some of the methods and tools used. Pits were often dug and animals were forced into them or into game corrals. Buffalo were driven over cliffs; game was stampeded by fire or run into water where they could be speared.

Following are examples of the various hunting tools and methods of hunting. A few are no longer legal these days, others are fairly ineffective, but some of them are just as effective as they were in the past. And some primitive tools are simply fun to make and use. In past sections we covered making axes, knives, bows, and arrows, which were used for both hunting and warfare. In this section we cover several other tools and methods.

Chapter
22

CLUBS, SLINGS, RABBIT STICKS, AND BOLAS

A club was probably humankind's oldest hunting tool and was used by most Native American tribes, including the Eskimos. Two types of clubs were used: the bludgeon and the slung club. The simplest bludgeon clubs were sticks that had the right heft and feel. Bludgeon clubs made of antler sections were also very common. This is especially true in the Northwest where they were carved from elk antlers. The jaws of bison and horses were also fashioned into deadly clubs. Worked stones were also sometimes lashed to antler, bone, or wood, although they then became more "axe" than club. If creating a club from wood, choose a heavy, dense wood that has a natural crooked shape with a bulbous end. Ash, oak, hickory, bois d'arc, and locust are all good choices. Many of these wooden clubs were carved into an effigy of the animal the hunter wanted to kill and they were quite decorative items.

Some West Coast tribes utilized a "donut" club. These had a wooden handle and a round piece of stone with a hole in its center fitted over the handle. A wedge held the stone donut in place.

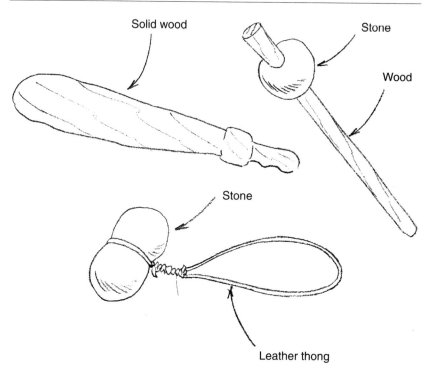

Solid wood

Stone

Wood

Stone

Leather thong

A club was mankind's first hunting tool, and a wide variety of club styles were utilized by the Native Americans.

Another type of club, as evidenced by artifacts, is the slung club, sometimes called a "braining" club. These consisted of a leather, sinew, or cord loop that held a round stone. These stones were usually fashioned with a groove around them or a hole for the sling to be tied to or to fit through. You can guess how these were used.

Thrown clubs, more commonly called "rabbit sticks," were very popular with the Southwest tribes. These rabbit sticks are some of the most common tools found in ancient graves in dry climates. Called the *kle-an-ne* by the Zuni, these are similar in shape to Australian boomerangs—except they don't return. Also

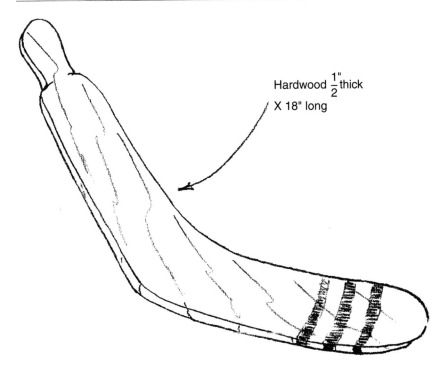

Hardwood $\frac{1}{2}$" thick
X 18" long

Rabbit sticks, shaped somewhat like boomerangs, were popular with some Southwest tribes. Rabbit sticks are thrown with the inside curve facing the quarry.

carved from a bent piece of wood, their tops and bottoms are flattened and a handle is shaped into their ends. In practice, the rabbit stick is thrown in the same manner as skipping a rock, with the inside of the curve facing toward the quarry.

Bolas were common tools that were typically thrown into a flock of birds. Both the Eskimos and California tribes utilized these very effective hunting tools. Bolas consisted of two or more weights, usually stones with grooves ground in them, but sometimes baked clay balls, that were fastened on cords. The Eskimos also utilized bone and ivory weights. In practice, the Native American bola was used in a manner similar to those of the an-

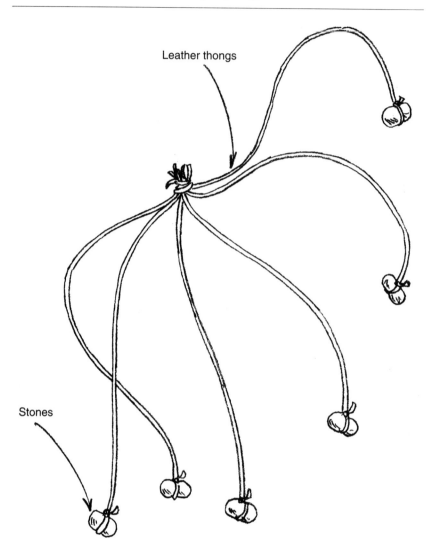

Leather thongs

Stones

Bolas, utilizing stone, clay, or ivory weights on thongs, were quite common and used to bring down birds from a flock.

cient Egyptians as well as the South American gauchos. The bolas were swung around the head, and then released into a flock, often bringing down several birds.

Chapter

23

LANCES, SPEARS, AND DARTS

The Plains tribes often used lances to stab buffalo from horseback. Lances were also common among other tribes to kill
game that had been forced into water. In this case, the lance was
often used from a canoe. Lances were made with a wooden shaft

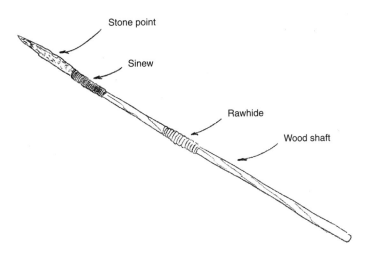

Stone point

Sinew

Rawhide

Wood shaft

*A lance was an especially effective tool used by the Plains tribes for hunt-
ing buffalo and other game.*

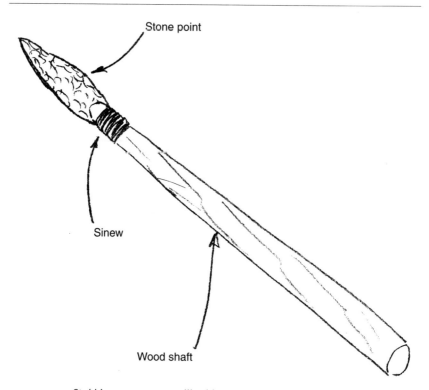

Stabbing spears were utilized by many pre-Columbian tribes.

onto which was fitted a bone, antler, or stone point. These are also fun to make and enjoyable to play with. You will need a stout sapling, about 1½ to 2 inches in diameter and about 10 to 12 feet long. Oak, hickory, and ash are good choices. Peel the bark from the shaft and smooth it with sandpaper or sandstone. Cut or sand the small end of the shaft to a rounded point, and then cut a slot to fit the lance point into place. These lance points were typically held in place with pitch and rawhide lashings. Bone and antler points were also sometimes pinned in place with hardwood pins.

There isn't much difference between lances and spears, although the latter were used both for thrusting and throwing. The pre-Columbian tribes utilized two types: the barbed spears, as discussed in the section on fishing, although they were also used on other game including birds and animals; and the non-barbed spears. Short stabbing spears and lighter-weight throwing spears were also used; the latter, however, were not quite as common. Short stabbing spears were, on the other hand, quite common and used for finishing off animals that had been trapped. The Eskimos often used short stabbing spears to kill swimming animals.

Spears and lances were probably the first "multipurpose tools." They could be used as lances, the handle cut down to use as stabbing devices, or the point removed and used as a knife, saw, or hatchet.

In these days of "automatic" or repeating guns, it's important to note that the ingenious Eskimos created a "repeating" spear. This consisted of a handle with a hole in the front, usually covered with a whalebone end. Similar to a harpoon, a smaller spear was set in place in the hole. The smaller spear was tipped with a sharp point. The spear was used to stab the victim, leaving the

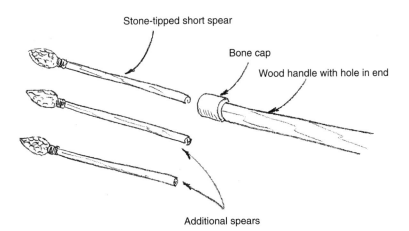

The Eskimos created "repeating" spears, or handles with separate smaller spears inset in a hole in the handle. The small spears stayed in the animal when the handle was withdrawn, and then more spears could be inserted and used.

smaller spear in place. Additional smaller spears, carried in a bag, could then be used as needed to continue to stab the quarry.

THROWN SPEARS

Thrown spears were also in use, although early man quickly figured out, that with all the energy needed to throw a large spear, they were fairly ineffective. On the other hand, smaller spears, actually darts, especially the bird darts created by the Eskimos and southwestern tribes, were extremely effective. These small spears were fairly lightweight, and often had multiple points with barbs, akin to fish spears. Fine bird bones, ground to a sharp point, were often utilized, lashing them in place with sinew. As anyone who has shot a wild turkey with a bow knows, an arrow quickly zips through it and the wounded turkey sometimes flies off. Modern-day archers have devised several means to keep the arrow in the bird. The early Native Americans also realized the problem and utilized a secondary set of prongs about a third of the length of the bird dart, to "impale" the bird and prevent the dart from

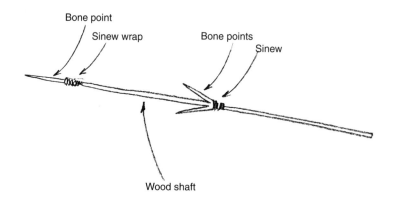

Small spears, or rather bird darts, were also quite common. Some of these had barbed points positioned on the shaft to prevent the spear from going all the way through the bird.

going all the way through. This slowed or hampered escape of the wounded bird. Most of the bird darts also had fletchings to stabilize their flight. Some experts suggest they were predecessors to the bow and arrow.

ATLATL

And this brings up the next very interesting hunting tool, the atlatl. Native Americans discovered early on that a spear could be thrown with much more force by adding an "extension" to it. These spear throwers were in use by the Eskimos, the Northwest, and some Southwest tribes. They were made of bone, antler, and wood. A variety of designs were utilized, although the basic concept didn't vary. An atlatl consists of a short piece of wood that has a hook or notch in one end and some form of hand hold on the opposite. The hand hold varied from a simple notch to those with finger holes. An atlatl is fun to play with. In use, the spear butt is fitted into the notch or socket, the spear and atlatl held separated with the fingers. As the atlatl and spear are brought forward, the spear is released, but the atlatl held firmly. Experts suggest the atlatl was of little use after the bow and arrow came into being in the New World, somewhere around A.D. 500.

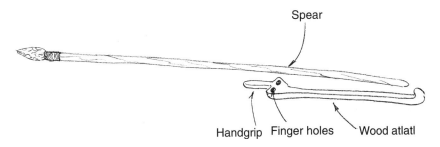

One of the most unusual hunting tools was the atlatl. Made of bone, antler, or wood, they provided more power for throwing short spears.

BLOWGUNS

Although more commonly associated with tribes of South America, Native Americans also utilized blowguns for small game and birds. There is no evidence, however, that the North American people utilized poisoned darts. Blowguns were made of any materials that could easily be hollowed out. Bamboo was a popular choice with the eastern tribes, such as the Cherokee. Elderberry was also sometimes used. Most blowguns were from 4 to 5 feet in length. The center was hollowed out with a stiff reed or limb. A red-hot ember pushed through the center helped to smooth the bore of the gun. The darts were 12 to 16 inches long and made of

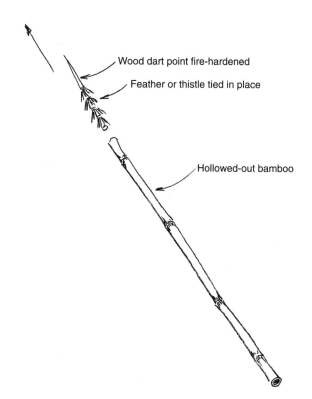

Wood dart point fire-hardened

Feather or thistle tied in place

Hollowed-out bamboo

Blowguns were common hunting tools of the eastern tribes, including the Cherokee. Blowguns were commonly made of bamboo with the center hollowed and smoothed.

a straight stick. Small diameter pieces of sumac, hazelnut, and dogwood were often used for the darts. The end was sharpened by grinding it down with sandstone and then holding it over a fire to harden the end. Fluffy feathers, or thistledown, were tied to the butt end of the dart with sinew to provide a "wadding" to close off the bore when the dart was shot. These blowguns were amazingly powerful and accurate hunting tools.

Chapter
24

TRAPS AND SNARES

The Europeans learned many of their trapping skills from the Native Americans. We already discussed traps used for fish, but the Native Americans also built traps and corrals for hunting as well. Game corrals were made to catch big game such as antelope and buffalo. Fire or simply numbers of people shouting and waving blankets and other items were used to run the game into the traps. Another common form of trap was the "pit." Deep

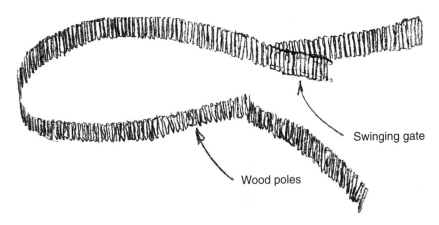

Swinging gate

Wood poles

Game corrals were used to capture large animals.

Pits dug in trails were also commonly used to trap animals.

holes were dug in trails, their tops covered over with thin branches and leaves. In many instances, the pit bottoms were lined with sharpened stakes.

DEADFALLS

Small game, as well as some big game, was also taken with deadfall traps. These traps consist of a heavy log or rock lifted up and propped in place by a stick or series of sticks. Deadfall traps are placed over trails and are also often baited. When the animal goes under the deadfall and knocks out the stick or sticks, the heavy weight falls, trapping and/or killing the animal. The weight of the deadfall depends on the size of prey. Quite often, branches, sticks, or stones were positioned to "funnel" or force the animal to go under the weight. Another type of deadfall utilized a weight and a hand-operated "trigger." In this case, the stick or sticks supporting the weight had a string attached. The trapper hid from view, watched the trap, and pulled the string to trap the game.

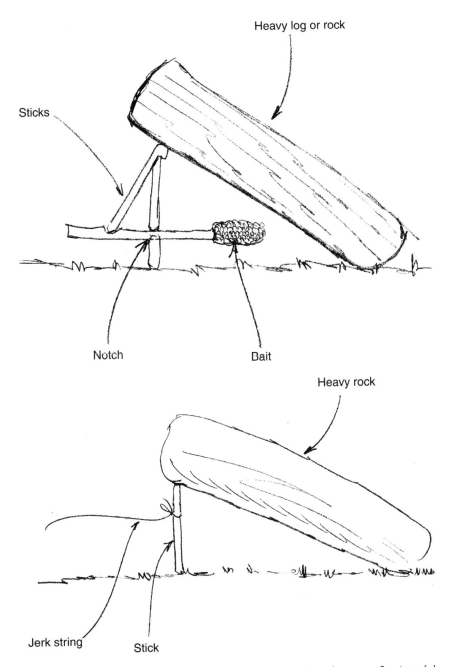

Heavy log or rock

Sticks

Notch

Bait

Heavy rock

Jerk string

Stick

A deadfall trap was a good method of taking small- and medium-size game. One type (a) utilizes an "automatic" trigger. Another (b) has a trigger activated by pulling on a string.

SNARES

One of the simplest traps was a snare, which was quite often used by the Native Americans for both small and big game. Even bears, elk, and moose were caught in snare nooses fastened between stout trees. When the animal ran into the snare, the noose tightened around the neck, eventually strangling it. Snares for small game consisted of a thin thong or, these days, a thin wire or cable. Two types of basic snares are used. The fixed snare is a loop set in a path, for instance, a rabbit run. Again, when the animal runs into the snare, it tightens, holds, and strangles it. Another type of snare is the "jerk-up." In this instance, the snare is attached to a heavy weight with one end hoisted up in place or to a tree limb or sapling bent to the ground. When the animal hits the snare, it pulls the snare of a notched trigger stick. This jerks the animal up in the air, killing it and, in the case of small game, also keeps it up and away from predators and scavengers until the trapper checks his traps. Sometimes bait was used to lure the animal into the snare. Both of these snares are very efficient, but illegal in many states and areas.

BIRD AND BOX TRAPS

Birds were often trapped in cages made of woven willow or other thin branches. The cages were set like a deadfall trap with a trigger stick that was either released automatically or was released when pulled by a jerk string. A string of corn or other bait leads the bird into a pile of bait located under the trap.

Box traps, although thought of as "modern-day" traps, were also quite commonly used by the Native Americans and the Eskimos. Thin slabs are fastened into a box. Thin wooden strips

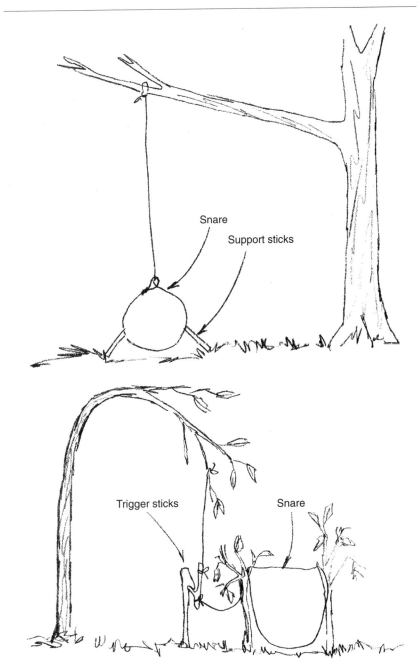

Snares provided a very simple means of obtaining both small and large animals. Two types of snares were used: a fixed snare (a) and a "jerk-up" model (b).

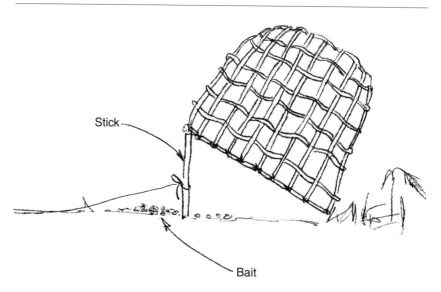

Bird traps made of woven thin branches were quite common.

enclosed one end, while a drop-down door operated by a trigger trapped the animal. These were used for rabbits, squirrels, and other small game such as woodchucks and marmots.

Chapter
25

CAMOUFLAGE, LURES, DECOYS, AND CALLS

The art of using camouflage, lures, decoys, and calls were also methods and tools utilized by the Native Americans.

CAMOUFLAGE

Camouflage was quite often utilized in stalking game. Many tribes used buffalo robes to resemble their prey as they stalked the big animals. A very simple method was for a hunter to sit astride a horse with the buffalo skin draped over him. The horse was then very slowly directed close to the herd. Wolf and coyote skins were also utilized since these predators were a normal factor of life near herds of animals and flocks of birds. Leafy branches or pieces of pine branch, bushes, grasses, and reeds were also fashioned to create natural camouflage for stalking game or while waiting to trap game. The Seminoles and other southern tribes used mud not only as a camouflage, but also as protection from mosquitoes.

LURES

Pieces of meat, nuts, or any food a particular animal or bird would want to eat were used as bait for traps or for luring animals in close enough to snare with a hand loop, to spear, or to shoot with a bow and arrow. Animal scent gland lures, in particular beaver castoreum, were also utilized. Castoreum has a very musky scent and will attract not only beavers, but also most other furbearers and predators as well. The lure can be used in conjunction with deadfalls or other traps.

DECOYS

Many tribes utilized various types of decoys for attracting game. Artifacts from the West Coast include reeds fashioned into the shape of waterfowl. Clumps of mud and rocks were also used to create waterfowl decoys. One Native American trick was, and still is, to prop up waterfowl that have been killed as "natural" decoys. Among artifacts are reed or willow cages used to hold live decoys, particularly pigeons, in order to attract other birds. The pigeon was "staked out" by tying it in place. Corn or other bait was scattered around the decoy and the hunter hid nearby. When other

Decoys, especially waterfowl and bird decoys were used by many Native Americans, in particular, the California tribes.

pigeons gathered, they were killed with clubs or caught with snares fastened to a long stick.

One of the more unusual Native American methods of decoying was used for hunting antelope. Knowing the innate curiosity of antelope, the hunter hid behind an object and waved a bright-colored flag or shield. The curious animal would eventually come close enough to be killed.

CALLS

Reproducing bird and animal sounds was a common method of attracting game close enough to catch or kill. Many of these sounds were made by mouth, simply imitating the bird or animal desired. In other instances, calls were constructed to imitate the various sounds. The Eskimos made "seal scratchers" of bone, antler, or wood, often with real seal claws fastened in place. These unique calls were scratched across the top of the ice, making one seal think another was on the ice.

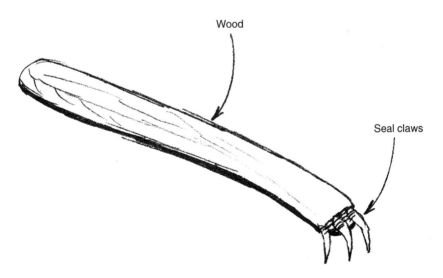

Seal scratchers, made of bone with seal claws attached, were used to scratch on the ice to make seals think another seal was around.

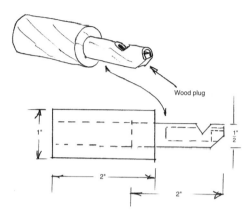

Waterfowl calls were used to create the sounds of widgeon, teal, and wood ducks.

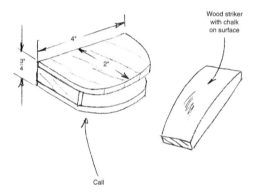

Box turkey calls were used by the woodland tribes.

Turtle shell/slate turkey calls are easy to make and use.

Waterfowl calls included whistles that replicated the sounds of widgeon, teal, and wood ducks. These were often made of hollowed wooden tubes.

Turkey calls were made of boxes created of thin slabs of wood. The box edges were then drawn over a piece of slate. Another type of turkey call is the box turtle call. The upper shell of a box turtle is used as the sounding box. The shell is removed from the turtle and well cleaned. A thin piece of slate is glued to the shell and sanded smooth. A striker is made from a stick about ¼ inch in diameter, whittled to a rounded end. The opposite end is inserted in a dry corncob. A 1-inch diameter section can also be whittled down to a thin handle, leaving a large knob on the end.

To use, the turtle shell is held and the striker dragged across the slate top piece to produce the different *yelps*, *purrs*, and *putts*.

One of the forms of calling that has come down through time is moose calling as practiced by the tribes in the North Country. Moose calls were typically made by rolling birch bark into a cone shape and lacing it together with basswood bark. Pitch was also sometimes used to help hold the bark together. The sounds produced replicate those of a cow moose and the calls are effective only during the mating season. The call actually is only a "megaphone" to amplify the sounds produced by the hunter. Several different call sounds can be produced. The most common begins with a sort of high-pitched whining note, increases in volume and lowers in pitch, and then ends with a short bellow. This is all done in one breath, and usually the sound is given several times. The hunter then stays quiet for a period of time. If a bull answers, the hunter gives another call. For further enticement, the last calls are quite often given in a lower "pleading" tone with the call held toward the ground. At the

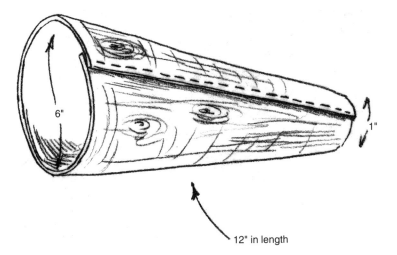

Moose calls, made of birch bark, were used frequently in the North Country.

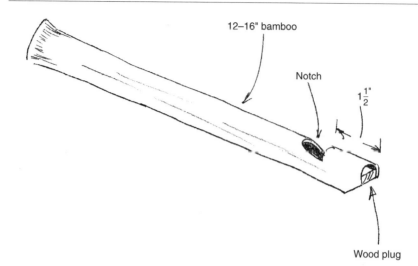

12–16" bamboo

Notch

$1\frac{1}{2}$"

Wood plug

Elk calls made of hollowed wooden tubes or bamboo are also fun to make and use.

same time, bushes and saplings are beaten with a stick to simulate the sound of a bull thrashing the brush.

Elk calls were also quite common. They were made of hollowed wooden tubes, with a plug in the end to produce a "whistle." It's important to have the plug sized properly and also to locate the plug properly in order to produce the three-note call of a bull elk. To produce the call, take a deep breath and begin gently blowing into the call to produce a low whistle. Increase the amount of air to bring up the volume and create the middle tone. Then, increase air pressure to create the final high, shrill note. Finish off with a series of grunts. Creating the enormous bugle of a bull elk isn't easy and it does take practice.

Deer calls were also popular. Some northeastern tribes made hollow wooden tube calls with a reed inside that produced the sounds of a bleating fawn.

Another type of call was used for several different animals and birds. It consisted of two thin pieces of wood holding a thin strip of birch bark or a blade of grass. The wooden strips are

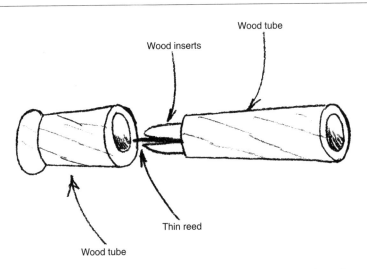

Deer calls utilize a hollow wooden tube with a reed inside to produce the sounds of a bleating fawn.

slightly hollowed in the center. When blown across, the shrill buzzing sound can be used to entice beaver, muskrats, and predators to come in for a closer look.

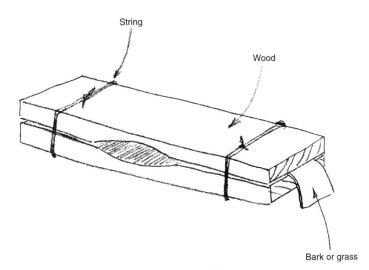

A simple call, made of two wooden strips to hold a blade of grass or thin piece of birch bark, can be used to call furbearers and predators.

Part VIII

Warfare

Warfare was prevalent among the Native Americans, although not in the same sense of organized fighting that we recognize today. Before the arrival of and conflict with the Europeans, most Native American warfare was more of what we'd call a skirmish. Battles were fought oftentimes simply because of the differences in languages. A common reason for battle was to steal women or horses—and to seek revenge for those insults. Some warfare was waged over goods and wealth, and quite a lot of warfare was precipitated by the trespassing of traditional tribal lands by other tribes. One of the most important reasons for warfare was honor. In many instances, a young man was not considered an adult, and was not allowed to marry, until he had gone on the warpath. Especially among the Plains tribes, a code of honor was followed. There were different honors for stealing horses and women, scalping, and even killing an enemy. Quite often, the highest honor was not for killing the enemy, but counting coup, or touching or slapping the enemy and then walking away. Particular feathers worn in certain ways denoted the honors the warrior had accumulated.

Although the morbid practice of scalping is much mentioned in modern literature, the Native American tribes didn't practice it as often as described until the arrival of the white man and the "competition" they introduced. Bounties were paid by the early Europeans for "dead Indians" and scalps were often produced as the proof of death. By the middle of the eighteenth century, as much as $134 was paid for male Indian scalps and $50 for female and children's scalps.

The Native Americans were extremely adept at what these days is called guerrilla warfare. They often struck quickly and inflicted as much damage as possible, then withdrew just as quickly. Many of the Native American chiefs were also extremely good tacticians.

Many of the weapons used for warfare were the same implements used for hunting and food gathering, with some exceptions. The bows and arrows were significant weapons and, until the advent of the repeating rifle, gave the tribes an advantage over muzzleloaders. The expert archers would shoot a dozen arrows while their enemy was reloading a muzzleloader. Basically, the same bows and arrows were used for warfare as was used for hunting big game. The making of those weapons was discussed in previous sections. Following are some of the "specialty" war weapons.

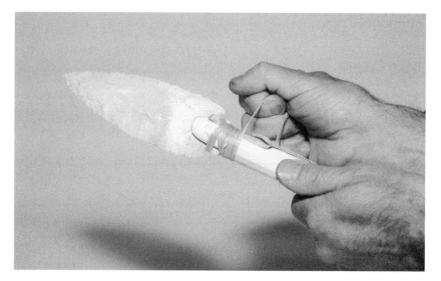

Making your own Native American–style spears and lances is fun and easy.

Chapter 26

LANCES, SPEARS, AND COUP STICKS

T he lance or spear used for warfare was also basically the same
as used for hunting. In most instances, however, the blades
were somewhat larger and longer. Lances and spears used for battle were, however, often highly decorated with feathers, fur strips,

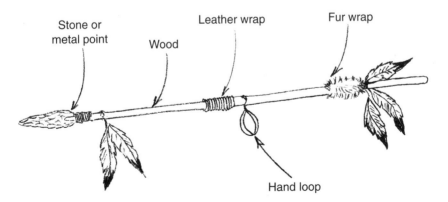

The war lance was a very special weapon of many tribes, especially the Plains tribes.
These lances were often highly decorated with feathers, paint, and fur strips. In battle,
the "dog soldier's" crook-tipped lance was stuck through a sash the warrior wore and into
the ground, pinning the warrior in place.

and paint. The Plains tribes "dog soldiers," as they were named by their enemies, were admired for their fierceness and bravery in battle. These warriors used one of the most interesting lances, typically fashioned with a hook or crook in the end and highly decorated. The warrior wore a long, brightly colored sash. If he was losing a battle, he would dismount from his horse. He would then stab the lance through the sash and fight to the death in that spot, or until another warrior rescued him.

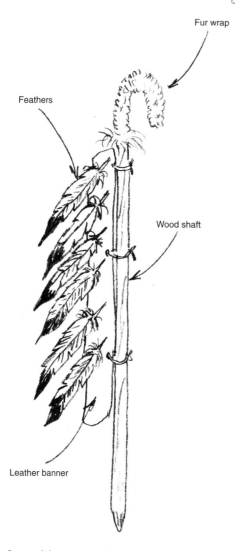

Stone points were the most common lance points, although in later years metal points were used. A war lance is an interesting decorative item, and a great use for those stone blades you've chipped. You'll need a sapling about 8 to 10 feet long and about 1 inch in diameter. It should be extremely straight and without any knots or blemishes. Remove all the bark and make the shaft as smooth as possible using sandstone or sandpaper. Cut a notch in the small or front end

Coup sticks were used to gain honor in battle by touching an enemy.

and fasten a stone point in place with pitch and sinew. Decorate the lance with feathers tied in place with sinew and painted bands. If you wish to make the end crooked, steam the lance and bend it over a form until it sets up as described in Section III, Chapter 3, on steaming a bow stave to create a recurve bow.

Pronounced "coo," a coup stick was used to touch or strike an enemy without killing him. This unusual weapon is basically a lance without a point and is also highly decorated. The coup stick is somewhat more slender and shorter than a lance and can be made from a sapling about ¾ to 1 inch in diameter and 4 to 6 feet in length. Both straight and hoop-end coup sticks were used. Some coup sticks were made in a banner style and these were often carried into battle much like any other war banner. The banner-style coup stick consisted of a length of bright colored buckskin or flannel tied to the stick. Strings of feathers were then tied to the outside edge of the banner.

Chapter
27

KNIVES, DIRKS, AND DAGGERS

S tabbing weapons were also used in battle and in ambush. In some cases, the day-to-day belt knife was used, but in most instances, everyday knives were more often used by

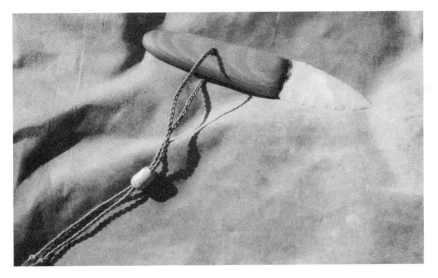

Just as in modern times, dirks, daggers, and knives were some of the most important weapons. Shown is a stone-point dirk made by Marty Horn.

women for butchering and other chores. Some weapons, however, were designed only for stabbing in hand-to-hand combat situations. These gruesome weapons were made of numerous materials including antler, bone, horn, wood, stone, and later from metal.

One of the simplest knives was made from a sharpened antler tine. An elk or large deer tine can be used. The antler tine is sawn off to about 10 to 12 inches in length. The point is sharpened with sandstone, and the sawn end rounded and smoothed. The handle is created by wrapping rawhide around the upper or large end of the tine. A "keeper" thong of buckskin is tied in place with the rawhide.

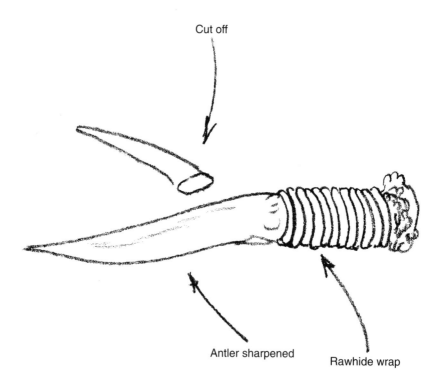

Cut off

Antler sharpened

Rawhide wrap

A number of stabbing weapons were utilized. A simple sharpened antler tine was very effective.

Wooden dirks or daggers were also extremely popular. They were simply pieces of wood carved into a dagger shape. The size varied from small up to some daggers that were a foot or two in length and almost "swords." The handles were often carved in a wide variety of decorations. If you intend to make one of these, you'll need a dense hard wood in order to maintain a "sharp" edge. Hard maple, Osage orange, and wild cherry are all good choices. Seasoned wood is the best choice, although you can make a dagger from green wood. The first step is to obtain the log. Split or saw it to remove the sapwood and create a "blank" through the center of the heartwood, the strongest portion of wood. Smooth up both sides to an even thickness. To make the Northeast dagger shown, enlarge the squared drawing and create the pattern. Transfer the pattern to the blank. You can cut out the outline using a saber saw, band saw, or coping saw. Or use a hatchet to rough out the dagger. The final dagger shape can be created using power sanders, a drawknife or spoke shave, a hatchet, or just a sharp knife. Once the shape has been achieved, sand the entire knife, handle and blade, as smooth as possible. Carve the butt decoration as desired. The handle can be left as is, or wrap rawhide or leather lacing around the handle to provide a better grip in slippery situations. Finally, sand and smooth the blade as fine and sharp as possible. Apply several coats of boiled linseed oil finish, buffing and polishing until the entire knife glistens.

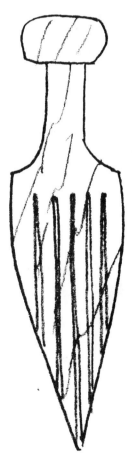

North Coast tribes often utilized a carved wood dirk or "sword."

My good friend Marty Horn produced a very interesting stone battle dirk. The short dirk is designed to be carried by a wrist thong. When you need it, simply snap your wrist upward and the thong flips the weapon into your hand. The first step is to

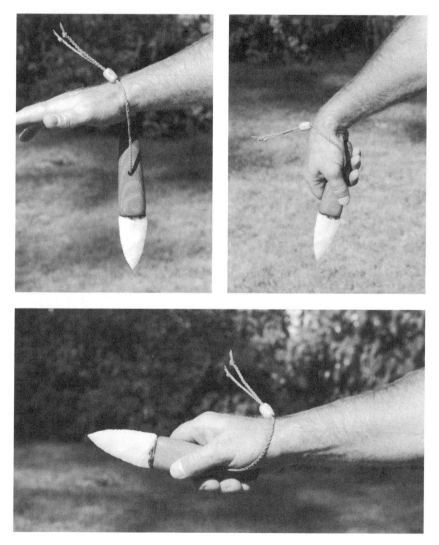

The stone dirk created by Marty Horn utilizes a wrist thong, providing instant readiness.

create the stone point, which is explained in Section I. A handle made of a smooth, dense hardwood is then created. Cut the handle to size and shape. The point is inset in a recess in the handle end. Bore holes to start the recess and then whittle the material out from between the holes to shape the recess to fit the butt of the stone blade. The blade is hafted into the handle using glue. Pitch or animal glue can be used, although modern glues can also be used. Gorilla glue is a good modern adhesive choice—it will glue just about anything. Drill a hole through the handle, about midway of the handle length. Insert a leather thong long enough to go around your wrist and leave about 4 inches on either end. Thread the thong ends through a short piece of antler with a hole in it for a keeper. The hole should be small enough to hold the thongs tightly while in use.

Chapter

28

CLUBS AND AXES

Some of the most common hand-to-hand combat weapons used by the Native Americans were battle axes and clubs. An ordinary hard, heavy stick was the first club. Later clubs were designed specifically for combat. A wide variety of clubs existed

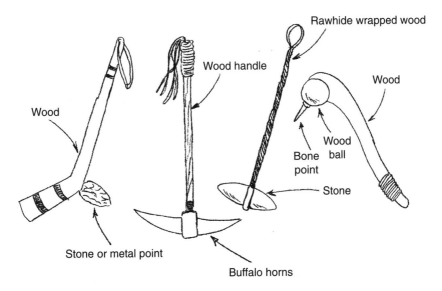

Battle axes and clubs were very common war weapons of all regional tribes. These clubs included ball-style woodland clubs, and the popular "gunstock" style used by both Woodland and Plains tribes. Brainer-style clubs utilized leather, stone, and buffalo horns.

from the eastern to the northern to the Plains tribes, depending on the materials available in the area. The jawbone of a horse was a common war club of the Plains tribes. The Woodland tribes utilized a "ball"-style club. The entire club was carved from a single piece of extremely hard wood. A single sapling was often used, the ball end being carved from the root.

Another extremely popular club style was wood carved into a shape similar to the European gunstock. This was used by both the Plains and Woodland tribes. The club often had wood, stone, or metal spikes inset in the end. These war clubs were usually highly decorated to show ownership and maintain the powerful "medicine" of the individual.

Some tribes also used "brainer" clubs, similar to those used for braining animals. These clubs consisted of stones tied to leather thongs. An extension of this was a stone with a wooden handle, all encased in rawhide and allowed to dry.

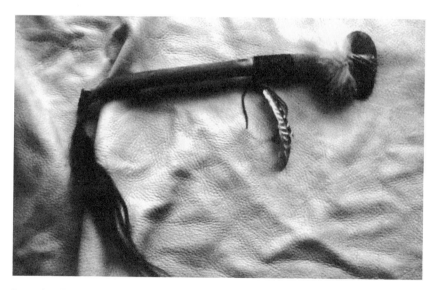

Stone hatchets were used for both work and warfare. Shown is a replica produced by Randall "Hutch" Hutchison.

Stone hatchets were also commonplace until the Europeans introduced the belt-axe trade tomahawk. The nineteenth-century pipe tomahawk was also a trade item that became extremely popular with both Plains and Woodland tribes. These pipe tomahawks are also the famous "throwing" tomahawks associated with the Native Americans. If you wish to make your own replica, the heads are available these days through a number of sources, including Dixie Gun Works. Both the handles and reproduction heads, including pipe heads are available. If you prefer to make your own handles, you'll need a piece of hard maple or

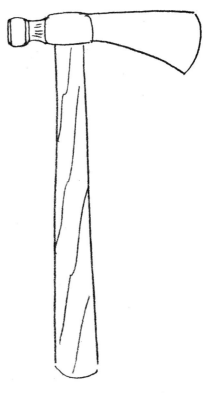

The nineteenth-century trade pipe tomahawk was a very popular weapon. The heads and handles are available to make up your own.

ash. Standard tomahawk lengths were 16 and 20 inches. The handles are rounded and tapered, then the head driven in place.

Chapter
29

WAR SHIELDS

One of the most interesting battle items was the war shield. These were primarily used by the Plains tribes. The Woodland tribes did not use them because they would have been a problem in the woods. Although these shields were used as "pro-

War shields were very personal items of the warriors. They were thought to have special magic for the wearer.

tective" devices, they were also considered to have magic power and were highly decorated and personalized. Not every warrior was allowed to carry a shield, only the more honored. Naturally, those carrying shields were the most evident and the most likely to encounter battle or be shot at. Capturing an enemy's war shield was one of the highest honors.

Shields were made from the chest area of a bull buffalo. The hide was cut into a round shape about a third larger than the finished shield was to be. The shields used by warriors on horseback were about 18 inches in diameter. Larger shields of up to 24 inches in diameter were carried by warriors on foot. The skin was dehaired, defleshed on the back, and in some instances the damp hide was placed over a mound of wet sand and allowed to dry into

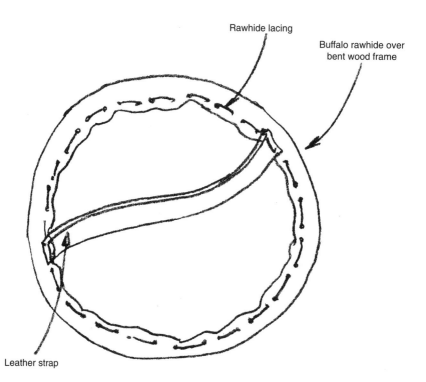

Rawhide lacing

Buffalo rawhide over bent wood frame

Leather strap

You can make up your own fairly easily with a section of heavy rawhide.

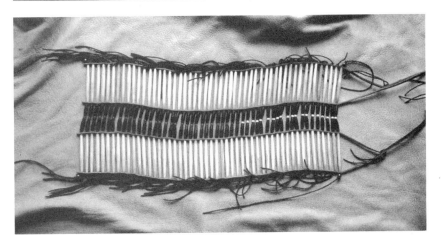

Bonepipe breastplates were an essential item of the Plains tribe's warfare. Shown is a replica produced by Randall "Hutch" Hutchison.

a curved shape. In other instances, the skin was left flat. A ring of saplings provided the outside support, with the shield lashed to the saplings and allowed to cure and dry. A buckskin holding strap was fastened to the back. The shield was then painted with the personal design of the warrior, often describing exploits or a vision. Feathers, furs, fringe, and other decorations were also added. A cover was sometimes used on the shield to protect it, and also to hide the symbols until the last minute of battle. War shields were the most valuable possession of the Native American warrior and were highly guarded.

You can easily make a replica shield from a piece of deerskin rawhide or cowhide. First, create a hoop from willow or other easily bent limbs. Lash the wet rawhide in place and allow it to dry and cure. Fasten the buckskin holding strap in place and then decorate to suit using acrylic colors and add other embellishments.

Index